Get out of the Boat
Walk on Water

by
Laura Charlene

Copyright © 2015, Laura Charlene
www.lauracharlene.com
Facebook Page; Laura Charlene Author

ISBN 10: 1511984937

ISBN 13: 9781511984935

Published by:
Inspired Perceptions

Purchase books at:
LauraCharlene.com

CreateSpace.com/5470205
KindleBooks.com
Amazon.com

Printed in the United States of America and the United Kingdom

Dedication

This book is dedicated to my two amazing children. My sweet daughter Kelly in Heaven, you were an inspiration for me to write this book. My best son Ryan, thank you for always supporting me. You both have given me precious moments of joy, laughter and love.

Blessings and Love,
Mom xoxoxo

Table of Contents

Introduction 7

Chapter 1
Don't Give Up Rise Up 11

Chapter 2
Get out of the Boat Walk on Water 19

Chapter 3
Extraordinary Kindness 27

Chapter 4
It's Not About Religion It's About Relationship 47

Chapter 5
Still Waters Run Deep 53

Chapter 6
Moses Sole Fish 63

Chapter 7
Faith Like Noah 71

Chapter 8
Prayer Parts Water 79

Chapter 9
Let the Healing Begin 95

Chapter 10
Three Crosses 119

Chapter 11
God's People 127

Chapter 12
Blessed In The City 135

In Closing 143

Acknowledgements 145

Contributions 147

Walk on Water Artist, Music and Lyrics 149

References 161

Introduction

We all have a story and it takes place moment by moment. Some of the story we hope to rush through or close our eyes and pretend it is not happening. We pray it goes away! When I was a child, my dad cursed Christ and my mom loved Him! My dad did provide for us. He worked a day job trimming trees for the city and a part time job at the post office in the evening. He worked hard during the week, then all weekend long he drank.

I have two incredible brothers, one older and one younger. My mom always tried to protect us. It was hard to see how my dad treated her at times. My mother was a prayer warrior. She was married for 53 years and continued to pray and stay with my dad.

During his later years my dad changed. We wish it would have been sooner. For his 70th birthday, our family hosted a huge party. Everyone got up and shared stories. Then at the end I was asked to speak. I was the MC. The first words out of my mouth were, "Dad I didn't like you very much growing up." The room became silent! You could have heard a pin drop. I continued, "Over the years I have grown to love you!" I gave my dad a big hug and kiss. Everyone cheered and applauded. He got up and thanked everyone for the party. He then announced, "I want to extend a personal invitation for each of you to come back here in thirty years when I turn one hundred."

He did not make that party! At age 82, he arrived in Heaven. Now he is walking on streets of gold! No matter what the trials, my mom kept praying for my dad all those years. My mother is also in Heaven now. My parents are dancing on streets of gold!

I have two beautiful children. My sweet Kelly girl is in Heaven. I am sure she is having long conversations with Jesus as she sits at His feet. My best son Ryan lives and works in California. He loves to be called my best son, even though he is my only son. I am very proud of him and his accomplishments. My children are treasures and gifts from God!

Some would say if I had known what I know today it would have been different. I believe that is the truth. For several years now I have truly known Jesus. I invited His Holy Spirit in my heart and life. His Holy Spirit dwells in me! I learned the power and authority we have through Him. I understand life's trials still come against us. Knowing how to prepare and fight those battles makes the difference.

I was born and raised in Minnesota around the Twin Cities area. I sold real estate most of my life. For several years I also owned and operated a business. I lived in Florida and Colorado the last few years. I love the ocean, the mountains and all the beauty God has created. America, the Land of Freedom! In God We Trust! Those are the words printed on our money. I also carry them in my heart and soul. Whether we our famous or not, we are all created in God's image. Jesus looks at our heart. God has a plan for each of us! His greatest commandment is to love the Lord thy God with all your heart, and with all your soul, and with all your strength! And the second is to love thy neighbor as thyself.

I love Jesus and want to follow Him! I try to be kind, love others and give Him my very best. I want to help people layer their foundation with principles for their life journey, doing it God's Way! The road of life has bumps, turns, curves and danger. Jesus smooths our path. He lights our way when we call upon Him. God makes the impossible, possible!

In our personal lives, at our jobs, in business and in the everyday world, we can have Heaven on earth when we abide in His presence! Reflect the glory of God! We all need to know how to do it God's way! He makes a path in the mighty waters so we can get out of the boat. We need to step out with Jesus! Then we can **Walk on Water!**

Don't Give Up Rise Up

Chapter 1

Psalm 37:4-5 Delight thyself also in the Lord; and He shall give thee the desires of thine heart. Commit thy way unto the Lord; trust also in Him; and He shall bring it to pass.

Disneyland is a theme park known around the world. The park is sometimes affectionately referred to as the happiest place on earth, other times, The Magic Kingdom. It isn't really about magic in the literal sense. Families enter a park filled with Disney theme rides, characters and music. They are excited, laughing and having fun!

The grounds are pristine. Employees scramble to pick up any paper that falls on the pavement. There are colorful lights and manicured shrubs shaped into Disney characters. Every concept is created to maximize enjoyment! It is a place not only for kids, but also adults of every age. Grown-ups feel like kids again. Happiness abounds!

As a teenager, Walt Disney was told by an art instructor he was not creative and did not have imagination. Walt had some 100 failures before he created Disneyland. One hundred trials and experiences!

Was each meant to improve and bring him closer to achieving his dream? Maybe failure is like a puzzle.

Every piece that doesn't fit gets you closer to discovering the one that does. Walt Disney never gave up! Noah spent 120 years building the ark. He never gave up!

Change is a part of life. We all experience it. Whatever life brings, we should not let it keep us from the changes we either need or want to make. As Ben Franklin once said, "When you're finished changing, you're finished." Change is needed inside and outside. Are we honoring God in the changes we make?

Steve Harvey is a well-known comedian. I have seen him change over the years, including the way he looks and dresses. He now wears designer suits with that prestige hankie in his left corner pocket. Most people address him as Mr. Harvey. They show him respect.

He also has a great smile! I can't help doing the same when I see it! Steve Harvey's path to success began in grade school. He wrote a book "Act Like a Success Think Like a Success." In the story his teacher could have killed his dream and his father could have buried it. Steve's dad chose to bring his dream to life! His dad encouraged Steve to speak the words in his life that he wanted and believe it! In my opinion, Steve Harvey became an "overcomer" at a very young age. He didn't give up, he rose up!

"Encouragement is awesome, it (can) actually change the course of another person's day, week or life."

- Chuck Swindoll

Romans 4:17 ......and calleth those things which be not as though they were.

Proverb 18:21 Death and Life are in the power of the tongue......

Proverb 23:7 For as he thinketh in his heart, so is he.......

At age 38, Mr. Harvey was on television for the first time. He was probably thankful God did not have him building an ark for a living! He said, "Today there is not a day that goes by you don't see me on TV." Steve Harvey worked hard, kept his dream alive in his heart and his faith in God!

I heard him speak on Trinity Broadcast. It is a Christian television network. They have a mixture of high profile ministers, speakers, singers, movie stars and special guests. It's all about God! Mr. Harvey spoke from his heart and described how he would introduce

Jesus if He was there that evening. In Steve's own words;

"Praise the Lord, my mother, a Sunday school teacher for 36 years, taught me that Jesus was going to come back one day! I believe that, through every piece of hard time I'd done had. You'll see me on tape and it don't look like I know him. Trust me, I know him every day. There is no way I would have gotten here without him. What I believe has got me here. This is real talk. So, if you will just imagine with me if I had the pleasure of bringing out Christ, this is just how I would do it. It ain't going to be the way you do it. You might think it's not just right but this is how I would do it.

Ladies and gentlemen, it is my honor to introduce a man who needs no introduction. His credits are too long to list. He has done the impossible time after time! He hails out of the manger in Bethlehem, Jerusalem by the way of Heaven. His Mother is still headlining in the Catholic Church today. His Daddy is the author of a book that has been on the best seller list since the beginning of time. He holds the record for the world's greatest fish fry. He fed five thousand hungry souls with two fishes and five loaves of bread. He can walk on water, turn water into wine, no special effects, no camera tricks. He has a head shot on every church van across the country. Even before the kings of comedy, he was hailed the King of all Kings. Ruler of the

Universe, Alpha and Omega, the beginning and the end, the bright and morning star. Some say he is the Rose of Sharon and some say he is the Prince of Peace. Get up on your feet, put your hands together and show your love for the second coming of the One and Only!!!"

When Mr. Harvey finished this brilliant performance, he was overwhelmed with emotion. Rightly so! His life has been a journey! He chose to rise up, not give up! Thank you Mr. Steve Harvey! I am so proud of what you achieved! You are still rising up and motivating others to do the same. You followed your heart! You keep moving upward no matter how hard the climb. You know God has your back!

Do you rise up or are you a complainer and impatient? Do you say God why me or God why not me! This is too hard, I give up! Don't take me out of my comfort zone. I don't like my job, but I'm afraid of change. I would like to go to school, but I'm too old. I love to sing, but can't carry a tune. Nobody likes me, I don't have any friends, I feel fat, I don't like the way I look, on and on.......

How does one get out of bed each morning when they are speaking this over their life? We have the power in our tongue to start changing our life through God!

"Yesterday is gone. Tomorrow has not yet come. We have only today. Let us begin."

- *Mother Teresa*

"God is looking for ordinary people empowered by Him to do extraordinary things."

- *unknown*

"How wonderful it is that nobody need wait a single moment before starting to improve the world."

- *Ann Frank*

"It is easier to prevent bad habits than to break them."

- *Benjamin Franklin*

"No one would have remembered the Good Samaritan if he had only good intentions."

- *Margaret Thatcher*

"If God is your co-pilot, swap seats."

- *unknown*

"My home is Heaven, I'm just traveling through this world."

- *Billy Graham*

"Even if you're on the right track, you will get run over if you just sit there."

- *Will Rogers*

"I'm not perfect. I'm never going to be. And that's the great thing about living the Christian life and trying to live by faith, is you're trying to get better every day. You're trying to improve."

- *Tim Tebow*

"Don't measure yourself with others, measure against your own strengths."

- *unknown*

"I believe the Bible is the best gift God has ever given to man. All the good from The Savior of the world is communicated to us through this Book."

- *Abraham Lincoln*

John 14:26-27   But the Comforter, which is the Holy Ghost whom the Father will send in my name, He shall teach you all things, and bring all things to your remembrance, whatsoever I have said unto you. Peace I leave with you, my peace I give unto you: not as the world giveth, give I unto you. Let not your heart be troubled, neither let it be afraid.

We must be careful about the words we choose to speak over our lives! Negative words like I can't, it probably won't happen, I'm a loser or I give up! Stop! We swing the door wide open for the devil to take over. Yikes!

Instead pray, "In the name of Jesus, I break off all negative words I have spoken over myself. Whatever is not from the Holy Spirit needs to leave now. Lord, refill me with your Holy Spirit confidence, wisdom, boldness, overflowing peace, joy and Your love in my life. Jesus, keep my eyes on You. Lord, I praise and thank You for guiding my life and all Your blessings!"

The Holy Spirit will teach us all things. Do we listen for His instructions and follow them? The Holy Spirit will bring us beyond what we can imagine. Take the limits off God! Our Heavenly Father loves us! He wants the best for us! There are many things we cannot do ourselves. There are no limits to what we can do with God! Let's speak into our lives what we know God has for us!

We have choices in life!
Stay in the boat and give up or.................

STEP OUT! RISE UP! WALK ON WATER!

Get out of the Boat Walk on Water

Chapter 2

Jesus said to Peter, "Come." He immediately got out of the boat and went toward Jesus. Peter walked on water until he took his eyes off Jesus. He was afraid of the wind and waves. Peter started to sink. He cried out to the Lord, "Save me!" Immediately, Jesus stretched forth his hand and caught him saying, "You of little faith why did you doubt?" (Matthew 14:31)

Like Peter, Jesus said to me, "Come." Jesus was calling me out of the boat and onto the water. He wanted me to attend Charis Bible College in Colorado. My home was in Minnesota. I was surrounded by great family and friends! I graduated high school but never attended college. I had a successful career in real estate. I was floating safely in my boat.

Jesus called and I stepped out. I graduated from Charis with a ministry degree. I then attended their year long business school, "Learning to Do Business God's Way."

Jesus says, "Come." What is He asking you to do? Join the church choir or help the homeless? It may be a task that is not in your comfort zone. Like Peter, we are trying to keep our head above water.

Do you cry out, Jesus help me? If you ask Him, He will stretch out His hand. Jesus will help you become a water walker!

Psalm 121:2 My help cometh from the Lord, which made heaven and earth.

"Jesus doesn't call the qualified, He qualifies the called!"

- unknown

When we ask Jesus and His Holy Spirit into our heart, our lives are changed! We need to give Jesus permission to use us. The Holy Spirit will do things through us that are far greater than we can imagine!

Galatians 2:20 (NKJV) I have been crucified with Christ; it is no longer I who live, but Christ lives in me; and the life which I now live in the flesh I live by faith in the Son of God, who loved me and gave Himself for me.

II Corinthians 5:17 (NKJV) Therefore, if anyone is in Christ, he is a new creation; old things have passed away; behold all things have become new.

Just for the record, writing this book was not on my bucket list. It was not in my comfort zone. I could have remained safely in the boat with my life jacket on. Jesus called me to step out onto the water and write this book. I am safe in His Hands. Why are some of us afraid to get out of the boat, while others walk on water? There are those who leap out of the boat and run to Jesus! How can we receive this relationship and all that God has for us?

Psalm 119:105   Thy word is a lamp unto my feet, and a light unto my path.

I always pray, "Lord light my path with a huge floodlight so I stay on the right one!

Psalm 119:133 (NKJV)   Direct my steps by Your word, and let no iniquity have dominion over me.

What shoes are you wearing? Are you prepared to walk in the direction He wants to send you?

Psalm 143:8   Cause me to hear Thy loving kindness in the morning; for in Thee do I trust: cause me to know the way wherein I should walk; for I lift up my soul onto Thee.

Do you listen for His voice? You can use Bible verses as prayers. Lord, cause me to hear You, know

Your way. Tell me where I should walk. I lift up my soul and life to You. Quiet me to hear Your voice Jesus.

Psalm 46:10 (NKJV) Be still, and know that I am God; I will be exalted among the nations, I will be exalted in the earth!

Psalm 29:4 The voice of the Lord is powerful; the voice of the Lord is full of majesty.

God speaks to us, let Him! Listen for His words, they may sound like our own voice. He may say it through someone else. The words may keep running over and over in our minds. It may seem we cannot stop it. When we listen, He opens doors for us to go through or closes doors He doesn't want us to walk through.

After I completed Charis Bible College, I returned to Minnesota. I own a home but had rented it out. I was staying comfortably at my brother Craig and his wife Katie's beautiful home for the summer! It is a home full of God. I had a private room and bath on their lower level walkout. It had a gorgeous wooded view. I enjoyed fabulous meals prepared by Katie. I was treated like royalty and surrounded by family, friends, laughter, joy, barbecues, birthdays and fun events. Our family's favorite card game is Skipbo. It is great for all ages!

I was led by God to write this book. I knew I needed to be alone with Him to focus on my writing. I prayed and He answered. God told me to find a quiet place. I made arrangements to meet my girlfriend Linda in Florida to search for rentals. God placed her in my life at ten years old. We have had the hand of God upon our friendship. On our journey, it is wonderful to have friends who encourage us and are in our corner. A true friend cheers us on!

Before the search even began, Linda called me and a door opened. She and her husband Bill wanted to bless me with their one bedroom condo rental in Panama City Beach. It is a fully furnished ocean front unit with an incredible panoramic view of the beautiful blue ocean water. I could hear the tranquil sound of the waves breaking. My balcony overlooked a white diamond sand beach. Glorious sunrises and sunsets embraced me with God's presence!

We have an awesome God! Praise His Name! Could there be a more perfect setting? He set me on water to write this book, "Get out of the Boat and Walk on Water!"

At the beginning of my first year at Charis Bible College, the worship team had auditions. It was always a desire of my heart to be able to sing. From an early age, I was told I could not sing or carry a tune. I was prompted by the Holy Spirit to sign up. I thought, "God are you sure you're talking to me? God, you know all things. Surely, you know I cannot carry a tune."

It was the last day to sign up. I still heard that small voice. I walked over to the sign-up table. Another girl was standing there. I said, "Are you going to sign up?" She said, "I'm thinking about it." I introduced myself and said, "I know you have a beautiful voice. It is not about us, it's all about Jesus. There are only two additional spots available. I'll take the eight o'clock slot if you want the one at 7:30."

As I walked away, I asked the Lord if I was just there to encourage the other girl. He did not immediately answer. I showed up early for my audition. The girl I met earlier sang like an angel. As I waited, I thought either God was going to perform a miracle on my voice or He had something He wanted me to learn.

I walked into the room. I was definitely out of my comfort zone. I was going to sing for the Director of Worship, Daniel Amstutz. He is a published songwriter and recording artist. He has served as a pastor and teacher over thirty years, while continuing to mentor ministry leaders. Daniel was very gracious. Most of my notes were off key. He never said anything negative. He tried to smile even though my singing must have been hurting his ears.

I finally stopped and asked, "Is there any hope for me?" He said, "You can sing, your voice just needs training." He then added, "I had another girl at your level. She became not just an average singer, but an excellent one. She took voice lessons. I'm going to write down "not now" on your audition form, leaving it open for a future one."

"When God is involved, anything can happen. Be open. Stay that way. God has a beautiful way of bringing good vibrations out of broken chords."

- Chuck Swindoll

I went home and thought about the many times negative words discourage us. We are told we are not talented, not smart enough, not good enough. Even worse, we sometimes believe them. God wanted me to learn to get out of the boat! Take the step! Hear His voice! Trust Him! Jesus will take us by His hand and help us walk on water! When it looks impossible, God will go before and make the way. Praise God!

Luke 1:37 For With God Nothing Shall Be Impossible!

Extraordinary Kindness

Chapter 3

Extraordinary Kindness? In the dictionary extraordinary is defined as exceptional and kindness as pleasant nature. An exceptional nature! To me extraordinary kindness means continual kindness. Now that is exceptional!

Ephesians 4:32 And be ye kind one to another, tender hearted, forgiving one another, even as God for Christ's sake hath forgiven you.

Some people's kindness comes natural. It seems they are kind all the time. I have given my cousin Diann the title, "Hostess of the World's Greatest Bed and Breakfast!" No, she doesn't own a bed and breakfast, but she should! She welcomes family and friends into her home with open arms. She loves when they stay overnight. Her guest room has a king size bed with beautiful quilts, comforters and pillows. The decor is warm, friendly and inviting. The weather can get to twenty below in the winter. Diann has an electric blanket on the bed to keep guests warm and cozy.

There is a table in her walk in closet with a darling little lamp, magazines, chocolates and caramels.

Thirsty? The recreation room refrigerator has every kind of beverage guests would want. At Christmas time, she has a beautiful plate full of Christmas cookies and treats!

Diann's lower level gives one the feeling of home. There are black and white photos of the family from days gone by, framed embroidered pictures and crochet lace doilies. We don't see much of that anymore, unless it is in an antique store. It reminds me of my Mom who is in Heaven now.

Diann's guest bathroom is like an elegant five star hotel! One will find any item they may need or have forgotten. There are beautiful smelling soaps, perfumes, hair spray, shampoo and conditioners. A towel warmer awaits for their morning shower.

Hungry? Ready for breakfast? Not only does the food smell and taste great, it is like walking into Betty Crocker's kitchen! Her darling sun filled bay window is accented by a delightful fully set table. The decorations in her home change with the season. It puts a smile on your face. It's like being in the pages of a storybook.

For larger gatherings, Diann sets the dining room for breakfast. The table is draped with an elegant tablecloth with lace and tied at the corner with ribbons. I love the little house butter dish. The fresh fruit looks so beautiful in the ceramic watermelon bowl. She serves rolls with caramel and butter oozing down the sides and a yummy breakfast bake of hash browns, cheese and bacon, all melted together. China, crystal and silver accent her beautiful table. Diann makes everyone feel like royalty. She makes it seems effortless, but I know how much work it is.

Her husband would agree. Diann treats him like a King! She is gracious and wonderful! A lot of people can cook, but not everyone has Diann's ingredients! She pours in kindness, stirs in happiness and sprinkles a lot of love on top! Love you Diann!

Galatians 5:22 (NKJV) But the fruit of the Spirit is love, joy, peace, long suffering, kindness, goodness, faithfulness, gentleness, self-control. Against such there is no law.

My girlfriend Laura is employed at a church with a very large congregation. One of her jobs is to manage the coffee shop. She is beautifully dressed. She always wears a smile on her face. The light of Jesus is in her and shines bright! Laura is fun to be around! She is kind to everyone! Her words encourage others.

Laura stays late even when she is not on the clock. She is willing to extend herself whenever anyone needs help. She doesn't get upset when others do not show up for their assignment. Laura keeps everything running smoothly.

Laura is just as caring when she is away from work. She is kind to restaurant servers and employees in stores. Her middle name should be "Kindness!" She sets a high standard to follow! You are amazing Laura! A gift from God! Love You!

Isaiah 54:10 For the mountains shall depart, and the hills be removed; but My kindness shall not depart from thee, neither shall the covenant of My peace be removed, saith the Lord that hath mercy on thee.

Why is it hard for some of us to be kind? Do we make excuses? Say we are too busy. We have recently gone through a recession. With the economy bad, employers expected greater customer service from their entire staff. Now it seems more employees try harder to be courteous.

Thank you! We all know the words. We like to hear them. When someone helps me in person or by phone I say, "Thank you for your extraordinary service. I so appreciate your "kindness!" I wait until the employee has finished. When I speak the words "extraordinary and kindness," they seem to flow straight to their heart.

The words put a smile on their face. If I am on the phone, I hear the change in their voice.

I have been doing this for a few years. The reaction is always the same. When someone hears the word extraordinary, they say to themselves, "Wow, no one has ever said that to me before. I want to live up to it!" They want to help me more! The words "extraordinary" and "kindness" raise the bar. It encourages them to be the best they can be!

Can we raise the bar for ourselves? Yes we can! Pray, "Lord I am available, make me usable. Help me be an extraordinary kind person!" Be kind! Help someone! Be an example of Jesus!

Sometimes we are nice but others choose not to be. My son Ryan was five years old. I had been teaching him manners. I wanted him to grow up to be a gentleman. He has! We were going into a shopping mall. Ryan held the door open for me and kept it open for the lady behind me. He had done this many times in the past. Everyone had always thanked him. He came up to me and whispered, "Mom, that lady did not say thank you." I bent down, put my arms around him and said, "Sometimes people don't say thank you. It isn't very nice. You be kind, you do the right thing!" I'm so proud of my son! It comes natural for him to show respect and be polite!

Matthew 22:37-39   Jesus said unto him, thou shalt love the Lord thy God with all thy heart, with all thy soul, and all thy mind. This is the first and great commandment. And the second is like unto it, Thou shalt love thy neighbor as thyself.

Things happen in life! Our human side gets upset. We need to ask God to change us. I remember standing in line at the grocery store. It was the Christmas season. My cart was overflowing with items. I looked at people around me. Their carts were also full. Most of them were far from jolly! With a very big smile and loud enough for them to hear, I said, "Isn't it great! It's so wonderful that we have the money for all this stuff. All we have to do is stand in line." A lady replied, "Yes, it sure is!" Another man said, "This is nothing. In the military, you are in lines a lot longer than this." Someone else added, "We are blessed."

It was my turn to check out. The cashier looked stressed. I started a conversation and she seemed to relax. I thanked her for her extraordinary service and kindness. I smiled and she smiled back. As she handed me my receipt I said, "Merry Christmas, God bless you." I have learned one person can make a big difference!

Proverb 31:26   She opened her mouth with wisdom; and in her tongue is the law of kindness.

My friend Mary lives in a rehabilitation retirement community. Day in and day out, breakfast, lunch and dinner, she does the same thing. Mary greets everyone with hello, a kind word and maybe a hug! It doesn't matter if they seem crabby. One day Mary asked me, "Do you think I'm doing enough for Jesus?"

Do we ever think we are doing enough? What we can do is give Jesus our best! Every person on staff loves Mary! When I come to visit, the staff knows who I am. She speaks highly of others. That is Mary! She is a person of extraordinary kindness! Mary, keep telling them about Jesus and loving them. You are a blessing! I love you!

Lori is an organizer. When I had a garage sale or moved, I could count on her. Lori is quick, efficient and a hard worker. She never complains if a task ends up being more work or takes longer than first thought. She loves to clean! She would come stay with me for a few days. Every time, Lori made my home spotless. She wanted to bless me!

Lori moved to a small town. The only job she could find was at the local casino pushing the soda cart. It was the last place she applied. No one else in town seemed to be hiring. She said to me, "As I push the cart, I pray for these people. I don't know if anyone else is praying for them."

Because of her great work ethic, Lori continued to advance. She was promoted to a managerial position. She had a great reputation. Fellow employees would seek Lori out when they needed prayer.

Lori continued to apply for other jobs and placed her trust in God. She now has a great job located only two blocks from her home! Her light of Jesus continues to shine. Lori is someone you can always count on! I love you Lori!

Psalm 117:2 (NKJV) For His merciful kindness is great towards us, And the truth of the Lord endures forever. Praise the Lord!

Forrest and Jane have a lovely cabin! My family had a cabin when I was young. Trying to keep it in shape was so much work. The upkeep, improvements and care were constant. The work involved in owning a cabin hasn't changed.

Forrest and Jane enjoy blessing their friends. They do all the work when they have guests at their cabin. It is so much fun! They have a jet ski, pontoon boat and a hot tub! They provide beautiful meals cooked on the grill by personal chef Forrest. Jane serves all the trimmings and desserts. Their generosity is overwhelming, whether at the cabin or elsewhere. I appreciate their extraordinary kindness! I love to be around them! I love you guys!

I have an older brother, Craig, and younger brother, Bill. I am the middle child and the only girl. I had my own bedroom. My brothers had to share a bedroom. Let's just say, they may not have been so extraordinary when I was younger.

I watched Bill in the summer while my mom was at work. We would walk to the lake when it was hot. One day, I kissed a boy at the lake. Okay, it was more than one kiss. I had to pay my little brother so he would not tell my Mom. I knew if she found out, I would not be able to go to the lake anymore.

My older brother Craig was Mr. Neat. Before going out for the night to an event or the roller rink, I would lay out the clothes I wanted to wear on the bed in my room. While I was in the shower, Craig would hang them all back in the closet. He did this every time. My mom and I told Craig to stop, he did not.

We did not have cell phones, video games or internet as kids. We had to create our own fun. We would play "bike ditch" with the other kids in the neighborhood. It was boys vs. girls. All backyards were off limits. One day we were having a hard time finding the boys. We heard them laughing and making comments how stupid the girls were. Stupid!?! Talking gave their location away. They were hiding in our back yard. Busted!

Craig was a big tease, especially when my girlfriends came over. One day, I was making a BLT with my girlfriend Judy. Craig grabbed the mayo jar and said to Judy, "Dare me to throw this?" He had a hand full of mayonnaise. She said, "You wouldn't dare." Wrong! Craig threw mayo in her face and hair. I stepped back as the mayonnaise fight began. I yelled to Craig, "I am not cleaning this up!" Yuk! What a mess that large jar of mayo made. It was all over the kitchen! They should have taken the fight outside.

As kids my brothers and I never did anything really bad. We were never arrested or took drugs. Our mom was a prayer warrior! Our lives were not perfect. I believe she prayed us through a lot of things.

At times when I was young I thought, "Mom is never moving in with me." How God changes us when we let Him. I was fortunate to have my mom live in my home the last two years of her life. Our mom was a blessing! All three of us welcomed her into our homes. My mom spoke into my entire life! She was extraordinary!

Times change! We grow closer. Now it feels like my brothers and I are all the same age. We are there for each other. I know the extraordinary kindness and love they have for me. I am welcome in their homes any time. I enjoy visiting and staying with them. Craig and Bill both have beautiful wives of God. My family is a treasure from Heaven!

II Peter 1:7 (NKJV)   to godliness brotherly kindness, and to brotherly kindness love.

Drew is my fix-it man. He takes pride in his workmanship. Drew takes the time to do a job right. His painting is perfect. There aren't enough hours in the day for Drew. Everyone wants to hire him. It is because he is honest, does quality work and charges a fair price. Drew has a good nature and wears a smile on his face. He is a joy to be around, another example of everyday extraordinary kindness!

Bruce is my insurance agent. He makes each customer feel like his only client. He is a phone call away when help is needed. He always has the solution. He has passed on these traits to the staff he and his wife have fully trained. When he is out of town or on vacation, one gets that same great care from his staff. I have known Bruce for years. The service never changes! It's always extraordinary! Bruce, thank you for your kindness!

Psalm 31:21 (NKJV) Blessed be the Lord, for He has showed me His marvelous kindness in a strong city!

Rick is a dependable friend. I am blessed he is helping me edit this book. He has a generous heart! He has given many hours of his time to complete this book. Rick always has a kind word and is available when needed.

He was a police detective. I have heard many of his stories. I noticed how he handled situations with people, especially youth. He was concerned and knew how to use his knowledge for good. Rick wanted to inspire and improve lives through his decisions and actions.

He wanted children and teens to grow and learn, rather than go in the wrong direction. He cared about their lives. These were not children of family, friends or his children. They were strangers to him.

I believe it is one of the ways we help change the world. Give back! Young people need values! For that matter, don't we all!

Rick thinks this is one of the less exciting incidents of his career. To me, it is a bold statement of "Nice does win!" A great lesson in truth! This is in Rick's own words, "I was working patrol. I had a few years on the job. One Friday night, another police unit got a call that a band was disturbing the peace. Then my partner and I got a second call at the same address reporting burglary suspects were there now.

The other officers were in the front yard talking to the owner. He was the father of one of the band members. He was standing over a gas powered mower.

I learned later from the officers that the band's music was loud. They heard it a block away. They tried to get someone's attention inside the garage where the band was playing. No one answered. They knocked on the front door. Then the resident appeared from the side of the house pushing the mower. The officers tried to explain it was late and the music was too loud. The resident interrupted and said, "The band is no louder than the lawn mower. Are you going to arrest me for mowing my grass?" He started the mower and cut a few feet of grass in the dark before turning it off.

I walked up and asked about the burglary. He said, "I called on them. I heard knocking and saw two guys in dark clothing. I thought they were trying to break in. Besides, they are trespassing. They can't just come on my property!" He continued, "I am an attorney. My kid can play anytime he wants. The band is not loud. Did you take a decibel reading to prove any different? Now leave my property."

It was not my call so when the two other officers turned and walked away, my partner and I did too. When we got to the street I said, "You know we will get another call from the neighbors."

The next day when I got to work, I referred to the City Code. There is an ordinance restricting noise. It states, any unreasonable noise no matter the time of day, is disturbing the peace. It is a misdemeanor. I armed myself with a copy of the section.

I went on patrol with my same partner. It was about five on Saturday afternoon when the call came in again about the band. I did not go directly to the house. Instead, I interviewed two neighbors on each side and two more across the street. All of them said it was too loud. Two neighbors were ready to move.

We went to the detached garage where the band was playing. I knocked on the metal door with my flashlight. I had to wait until the song ended to get their attention. The teenage son of the lawyer came out the side garage service door. I said, "Go get the other band members, I want to talk to all of you now."

He went back in the garage. The others came out, he did not. He went into the house instead. I suspected he was calling his dad. I went inside and he was on the phone. I said, "Hang up, you are under arrest." He said,

"I'm talking to my attorney." I advised him he could call back after he was booked. That was the Law!

I walked with him to where the others were standing with my partner. I said, "You are all under arrest." I read the section. They had a look of disbelief and started asking for a chance. They said the attorney told them the police could not do anything and they could play as loud as they wanted.

I said if we carried through with the arrest, their instruments and equipment would be seized as evidence of the crime. When the case was over, a judge would decide whether to release the property back to them.

Now they were really pleading. They did not want to chance the loss of their instruments. I wanted them to understand there were consequences to choices. I told them we were not going to arrest them. We wrote down their names and information, discussed insulating the garage, turning down the volume and practicing after school when many of the neighbors were still at work.

I came into work the next day. My sergeant told me Mr. Attorney had been on the phone all day Sunday. He complained to city council members, the Mayor's office, Chief of Police and many others. That's not easy to do on a weekend. A complaint was taken, but he refused to be interviewed.

A month later, I was served with a civil lawsuit alleging false arrest, false imprisonment, trespass, etc. Mr. Attorney was asking for 32 million in damages.

Every few months for the next couple years my partner and I were served with written questions Mr. Attorney filed with the court. For example, he asked, "What about a flute is like a machine gun?" Yes, most of the questions made no sense. We would meet with the city attorney to answer them. He later told us he was unable to represent us. Mr. Attorney was now suing him too.

Finally, the trial! My partner and I were sitting at the counsel table as defendants. He had requested a court trial instead of a jury trial. The trial was a circus. He screamed at his own co-counsel and even faked a heart attack.

Mr. Attorney called each band member to the stand. Imagine his surprise when they all told the truth. They said he was wrong. He urged them on to play loudly. Each of them said he later asked them to say they were manhandled and roughed up by the police. Instead, they described our professionalism and friendliness.

Then the most amazing thing happened. He called his son to the stand. His son testified the same as the other band members. He said he knew the music was too loud but his dad told him it was all right. His son said we were nice to him. He said he was a plaintiff only because his dad made him. Mr. Attorney alleged his son was beaten, unable to sleep, had nightmares, etc. The son said none of it was true. How re-freshing it was to hear these young adults tell the truth!

The judge reached a decision. It was time to face the music! He awarded Mr. Attorney zero, zip, nada! The judge then looked at us and said, "I'm giving you an order. If you receive another disturbing the peace call at that address, you are to knock the door down if there isn't an immediate answer and arrest him, indicating Mr. Attorney. This is a court order, you do not need a warrant!" The judge ordered Mr. Attorney to pay all court costs!

I wanted to stand up and cheer for the judge! Why is it those who are wrong keep pursuing a victory. They want us to wear down, react or give up. They yell, harass, call or text us over and over again. They are trying to get what they want. Their actions rob us of our peace. They can drain the life out of us. Don't let them!

Give the battle to the Lord! Call upon our Heavenly Father. Remember these words, "Help me Jesus!" Jesus never leaves us He wants to hear from us. Receive His peace! With God all things are possible. Pray for wisdom. Ask Jesus to soften their heart. Pray for them.

What does God want us to do? Listen for His voice. Remain in His presence.

Make sure you have your armor on. Remember God parted the Red Sea with a person just like us holding up a simple piece of wood. Think what he can do for you!

Psalm 35:1 Plead my cause, O Lord, with them that strive with me: fight against them that fight against me.

John 10:10 The thief cometh not, but for to steal, and to kill, and to destroy: I am come that they might have life, and that they might have it more abundantly.

Don't let the devil rob your peace. Our human side may want to react. Rick remained calm, professional and showed the teenagers he cared. They chose truth over lies! I believe it may have changed the course of their lives.

There are no excuses for not doing the right thing. God did not ask us to build an ark. He did say to be kind to one another. Start with a smile! Add compliments! Kindness makes a difference in the lives of others. Kindness gives people unspeakable joy!

Be a person of continual Kindness!

That will make you Extraordinary!

It's Not About Religion It's About Relationship

Chapter 4

A few years ago, I went on vacation with my girlfriend Virginia. It was a very peaceful, relaxing and fun time! What I remember most from the trip was a small very old Polish Catholic Church. It was the kind with the irreplaceable stained-glass windows, wood carved pews that last a lifetime and a priest who was well fed by his congregation!

We attended a special weekday service that featured a guest singer my friend Virginia wanted to hear perform. About fifty people were in attendance. The guest singer sang some beautiful worship songs. Then the priest started his sermon. All of a sudden, he stepped down from the pulpit. He walked up and down the aisle as he continued his lesson.

"I've got news for you Catholics," he said. "There will be Baptists in Heaven, Lutherans in Heaven, Methodists in Heaven." He continued until he had named almost every major Christian religion. He then said, "It's not about religion, it's about your relationship with Jesus!"

It's Not About Religion It's About Relationship

Do you have a relationship with Jesus?   Do you know Him?   Do you talk with Him? Do you listen? Do you hear His voice? Do you walk with Him?   Do you read His word? Do you know what a really great relationship is? Have you had one? In a relationship with a friend we talk, we listen, we get together.

Relationship:

It is not what you can get, but what you give.
It is more about the other person than you.
It is caring and loving your friend more than yourself.
It is stepping out in faith and being a best friend.
It is supporting friends when others come against them.

Ecclesiastes 4:9-10   Two are better than one; because they have a good reward for their labor. For if they fall, the other one will lift up his fellow; but woe to him that is alone when he falleth; for he hath not another to help him up.

I remember a person who was in my life several years ago. I tried to be her friend. She had no others. One day, she asked me why I had so many friends. I said, "My friends aren't perfect. Neither am I. You have to love people for who they are." I said to her, "You seem to find fault with everyone you meet. Start looking for the good in people, you will find it!"

It's Not About Religion It's About Relationship

We are all a work in progress. Hopefully, we are trying to get better. I recall the last time we were at dinner with a couple of my other friends. I thought she was having a wonderful time. Afterwards, the only words I heard from her were negative. She commented that one of them talked too much. She criticized what they were wearing. I viewed the evening differently. I was glad someone was carrying the conversation. My friends were funny and I laughed a lot.

I realized I was a crutch for her. There was a reason she had no social life. She needed to meet people, join church groups, volunteer. Simply put, get involved! More importantly, she needed to change. If you want friends, you have to be a friend. God does the changing and the fixing when we choose to let Him. We cannot change anyone but ourselves.

We can be drained by people who do not want to change. Sometimes we have to step away and surrender them to God. We should continue to pray for them. We are accountable to God and responsible for our own actions. If we continue to be their crutch, they may not be motivated to change. They may think they don't need God's help. When we stay close to God, He will direct our paths.

49

It's Not About Religion It's About Relationship

We all need a relationship with Jesus. He is our very best friend and that's the way it should be! Start your day by saying, "Good morning Jesus!" We can talk to Jesus about anything and everything. He has our best interest at heart. No one loves us more! His love is everlasting!

Hebrews 13:5 (NKJV)..............I will never leave you nor forsake you.

A relationship with Him is important to help us grow and lift us up. We need to walk with Jesus every day! You may be thinking, I still have to live in the real world. You are right. Just because we know Jesus, things still come against us. We may have a bad job or boss, a dishonest business partner, a divorce, sickness or the death of a loved one to deal with. We have to be on earth right now, but not live here.
We step into the heaven on earth when we know Jesus.

Romans 12:2   And be not conformed to this world: but be ye transformed by the renewing of your mind, that ye may prove what is that good, and acceptable, and perfect, will of God.

We can be bitter, wallow in self-pity and sadness, or crush the devil under our feet and take our authority in Jesus Christ!

Isaiah 54:17 (NKJV) No weapon formed against you shall prosper, And every tongue which rises against you in judgment you shall condemn. This is the heritage of the servants of the Lord, And their righteousness is from Me, Says the Lord.

In the name of Jesus, break off whatever is coming against you. Negative words you have spoken over your life or the life of someone else. Pray, "God overflow me with Your Holy Spirit wisdom, peace, love, joy, knowledge, understanding and boldness in Christ. I thank and praise You Heavenly Father!"

Have you ever wanted to get better at something? For example, dancing, a sport or playing an instrument? Did you read about it? Talk to others who were more knowledgeable? Did you ask questions and practice, practice, practice?

We need to do the same when we want to know Jesus and be close to Him. Read His word! Go to church and places where we can hear and learn more about Him. Ask questions! Talk to Jesus! Listen to His voice! Learn from His Holy Spirit! Spend time with God! He changes us!

What If We Talked To God As Often As We Text!

What If We Were In His Book As Much As Facebook!

My prayer is for you to have a relationship with Jesus. I pray your heart is open to the Holy Spirit! Seek Him! Know Him! Trust Him!

I John 1:7 But if we walk in the light, as He is in the light, we have fellowship one with another, and the blood of Jesus Christ His Son cleanseth us from all sin.

Have a relationship with Jesus!

Still Waters Run Deep

Chapter 5

Psalms 23 The Lord is my shepherd; I shall not want. He maketh me lie down in green pastures: He leadeth me besides the still waters. He restoreth my soul: He leadeth me in the paths of righteousness for His name's sake. Yea, though I walk through the valley of the shadow of death, I will fear no evil: for Thou art with me; Thy rod and Thy staff they comfort me. Thou preparest a table before me in the presence of mine enemies: Thou anointest my head with oil; my cup runneth over. Surely goodness and mercy shall follow me all the days of my life: and I will dwell in the house of the Lord forever!

Three very strong friends come to mind when I think of Psalm 23. They walked through the valley of the shadow of death. My friends had a choice. Would they let Jesus comfort them? Would they let Him lead them to still waters? Would each of them let Him restore their soul?

I met my friend Ginny when I sold her a townhome in the community where I lived and worked. There is so much joy about her. She always speaks kind encouraging words. She is filled with laughter. Ginny has a positive attitude and a never ending smile! Her fashionable apparel accents her energetic personality!

Ginny had moved back to Minnesota from Florida to be close to her children when her husband became ill. He was sick for a very long time before he went to Heaven. Her wonderful husband was the love of Ginny's life. Sadly, I never had the pleasure of meeting him. How difficult to go through death and grieving while trying to stay strong.

Ginny also told me her daughter had died at 22 years old in a snow mobile accident. Ginny describes Debbie as her precious little girl. She loved life and had a bubbly personality. It sounds to me like she was a reflection of her Mom. Debbie had a six month old baby when this happened. I never would have known the pain Ginny suffered if she had not told me. It was so very heartbreaking!

Ginny is eighty one. Her age is no secret! When she turned 80, the major grocery chain where she still works had a party in her honor. Her birthday was covered by the press.

Ginny went to work for the grocery chain following her first retirement. She has worked in the flower gift department for 15 years. The company has transferred

Ginny to different stores. Each store doubled their business after Ginny arrived. She takes personal interest in her customers. When the economy slumped, her store cut back employees. They kept Ginny. The reason went beyond her exceptional sales ability. She was responsible for the high morale and joy in the store!

Upper management, the store managers, employees and the customers love her. She knows everyone's name, as well as their kid's names and ages. Ginny has two more children, five grandchildren and ten great-grandchildren. Now Debbie's six month old baby is grown with a baby of her own. Ginny is that amazing fun Grandmother every kid wants!

Michele is a beautiful woman with the heart of an angel. We both had careers in real estate. At one time, she was also my manager and I enjoyed working with her. Michele is still in real estate. She is well respected in the industry. Integrity, knowledge, experience and a caring attitude come natural for Michele. She has a smile that lights up any room. Her heart is packed full of generosity!

Michele had a set of twins, a boy and a girl. She also has an older son. Brett, one of the twins, was 13 at the time. He was sitting at the kitchen snack bar. He said to Michele, "Mom, if I die tomorrow, I just want you and Dad to know I've had the best life!"

A few weeks later on a sunny afternoon, family and friends gathered for a high school graduation party for her older son. Brett was among the attendees along with his twin sister. It was held at his dad's place of business, a landscape company called "God's Country." Brett asked to use the golf cart to drive around with one of his friends. He had driven the cart many times before.

What happened next is unclear. The cart may have mishandled or Brett took a turn too sharply. Either way, it tipped over on top of him. He was not moving. His friend ran and got help. The medical report indicated Brett died instantly. It is a moment etched in your memory forever. You can't breathe. It does not feel real. Your heart breaks! Can it ever be repaired?

Less than a year later, the family was at a cabin belonging to Michele's in-laws. Her husband didn't feel well and went home early. She arrived soon after with their children. Michele found her husband dead in his home office. Her heart again was shattered.

The following winter, Michele found out she had breast cancer. In baseball, the rule is three strikes and you are out. Not Michele! She had suffered the death of her child and husband. She had been diagnosed with cancer. Now she faced financial uncertainty. She had no idea of how to run a landscape business. It had to be sold! Michele felt she was back at "first base" and struggling to go on.

Michele prayed and wiped the tears from her eyes. She knew she had to be strong for her kids. She had a choice to give up or rise up. Jesus is the only physician who heals broken hearts. God said there will be valleys and He will never leave us.

Michele chose to rise up! The landscape business sold that winter for cash. Her cancer was healed. Michele was recently blessed with her first granddaughter, born to her oldest son and daughter-in-law. She team sells real estate with her beautiful daughter. Michele and her new husband of five years are making memories together.

Susan has a kind heart and a loving spirit! She has a beautiful face with a darling dimple smile. Susan's complexion glows. She has great expressions and I love her voice. We could be sitting around doing nothing and laugh and laugh! Susan is hard-working, eager to help and smart!

Still Waters Run Deep

Susan comes from a large family. She loves gathering with them and her many friends. Susan has two daughters and one son. I have a daughter and son. Her son John and my son Ryan were born three months apart. They were like brothers.

John was 28 years old. He and his wife had a New Year's Eve Party. After the party, they went out with their friends. They left together in the other couples car. Prior to leaving, they all discussed staying at a hotel that night. At the end of the evening, the couples decided to return home. Two of them did not drink alcohol and the other two had consumed very little.

All four returned to John's home and went inside. Almost immediately, there was a knock at the front door. John opened it. Two men with guns entered by force. They ordered them all to lie face down on the floor. The intruders asked where the safe was located. John repeatedly told them they did not have one. The intruders insisted they did. John said, "We don't have a safe, we have laptops, wallets, rings."

One of the intruders took John's wife out from the living room to look in other rooms for valuables. He then forced her to the bedroom at gunpoint. We don't need to speculate what was going through John's mind, a man that had "Jesus is my hero" on his Facebook. He loved his wife more than life itself. He jumped from the floor to protect her. His thoughts were not about his safety, they were only of her. One of the intruders fired several rounds from his gun. John was struck twice, once in his stomach and once in the neck. The bullets did severe damage and never exited his body.

After the shots were fired, the two intruders ran out of the home. John's wife hid in the closet. She realized she had her cell phone in her pocket and dialed 911. She did not know that John had been shot.

The other couple got up and ran to lock the deadbolt on the front door. At the same time, the intruders decided to come back. They attempted to enter the door which was yet to be secured. The couple was struggling to fully close it. One of the intruders managed to keep the door partially open. The hand with the gun in it was protruding inside. It prevented the door from fully closing. There was a fight back and forth to push the gun out. Hearing sirens approaching, the intruders finally fled to a waiting vehicle and left.

In the meantime, John stood back up. He was badly wounded. A large pool of blood marked where he had first fallen. John attempted to reach every hallway door. He was searching for his wife. His bloody hand prints were found at every doorway. He was unable to call out to her due to the severe wounds he sustained. He finally collapsed in front of the Christmas tree.

John was rushed to the hospital. Doctors tried to save him. In the early morning hours on New Year's Day, he met Jesus. John had followed in his Heroe's footsteps. He died trying to protect his wife.

John 15:13 (NKJV) Greater love has no one than this, than to lay down one's life for his friend.

Susan was still in route to the hospital when John passed. Even before Susan knew who the murderers might be, she forgave them for killing her son. She told me, "I didn't want to be in my own prison."

Police arrested suspects in John's murder following a ten month investigation. Susan attended the two years of court proceedings that followed. She relived the event over and over again. After motions, a mistrial, legal maneuvering and a second trial, the district attorney was unable to get a conviction. Susan had listened to the testimony. She feels the accused were guilty. Her reaction, "I'm not their judge, God is."

Susan recalled something she had once heard, "Unforgiveness is like poison, you drink it, but you want the other person to die." (Margaret Stunt) Susan focused on John's goodness and her experience as his mother. "It was God's gift to me," she said. She forgave the men that murdered her son and she was set free!

It's not easy to forgive! I think we have all had times in our life we needed to forgive someone. There are times we don't feel like forgiving.God commands us to forgive. If we don't, we are held hostage by bitterness, hate, sadness, pain, etc. When we do, it is a weight lifted. We must forgive! We cannot let unforgiveness block anything God has for us.

Mark 11: 25-26 (NKJV)   And whenever you stand praying, if you have anything against anyone, forgive him, that your Father in Heaven may also forgive you your trespasses. But if you do not forgive, neither will your Father in Heaven forgive your trespasses.

You have read the stories of three amazing women. Now answer these questions. Did you feel they embraced the comfort of Jesus? When He led them to Still Waters, did they trust Him? Did they lie back in the water and float in the arms of Jesus? Did you feel their souls were restored? Did you shut your eyes and see Jesus carrying them through the valley and wiping their tears away? Do you believe goodness and mercy shall follow them all the days of their life and they will dwell with the Lord forever? If this was you, would you give up or rise up? These women didn't give up or let death destroy them.

They empowered themselves to rise up through God's Grace. Amen!

Moses Sole Fish

Chapter 6

I asked God, "How can I explain to others the power and authority we have in Your Spirit? Your word says You have given us the same power that You gave Jesus on the cross."

Romans 8:11 (NKJV) But if the Spirit of Him who raised Jesus from the dead dwells in you, He who raised Christ from the dead will also give life to your mortal bodies through His Spirit who dwells in you.

A few days later I heard about a little flounder that lives in the Red Sea called the Moses Sole Fish. I often say, "God parted the Red Sea, your problem is nothing for Him!" I found information and great videos of this little fish on the internet. The fish camouflages itself at the bottom of the sea. It is almost transparent.

Sharks normally feast on flounder. They will not eat the Moses Sole Fish. Researcher discovered the reason! God gave this little fish a defense system. It naturally secretes poisonous toxins from its glands when in danger. These toxins cause the jaws of a shark to be paralyzed! God is amazing! He created the Moses Sole Fish and gave it a way to protect itself from its natural enemy. God also offers us protection! God gives us power and authority through His Holy Spirit. We need to learn how to use it!

Put On The Whole Armor Of God

Ephesians 6:10-19 (NKJV)

Finally, my brethren, be strong in the Lord and in the power of His might.

Put on the whole armor of God, that you may be able to stand against the wiles of the devil.

For we do not wrestle against flesh and blood, but against principalities, against powers, against the rulers of the darkness, of this age, against spiritual hosts of wickedness in the heavenly places.

Therefore take up the whole armor of God, that you may be able to withstand in the evil day, and having done all, to stand.

Stand therefore, having girded your waist with truth, having put on the breastplate of righteousness.

And having shod your feet with the preparation of the gospel of peace.

Above all, taking the shield of faith with which you will be able to quench all the fiery darts of the wicked one.

And take the helmet of salvation, and the sword of the Spirit, which is the word of God;

Praying always with all prayer and supplication in the Spirit, being watchful to this end with all perseverance and supplication for all the saints.

And for me, that utterance may be given to me, that I may open my mouth boldly to make known the mystery of the gospel.

Let's examine the words in Ephesians 6:10-19 more closely. The words are defined in the dictionary. Be open to the Holy Spirit to speak wisdom, knowledge and understanding in you!

Be **strong** in the Lord!
Strong; **powerful, zealous, firm, solid, might, power, authority.**

And in the **power** of His might.
Power; **authority, one that has control.**

Put on the **whole** armor of God,
Whole; **having all the proper parts. Free from defect or damaged. Not scattered or divided. Complete.**

That you may be able to **stand against**
Stand; **position, view point. Be at rest in an upright firm position.**
Against; **in opposition to, facing, as to touch or strike.**

The **wiles** of the devil.
Wiles; **a trick, intended to ensnare or deceive.**

For we do not **wrestle** against flesh and blood,
Wrestle; **to struggle for control, to throw down the opponent.**

But against **principalities**, against powers, against the rulers of the **darkness** of this age,
Principalities; **the position, territory, or jurisdiction of a prince.** Darkness; **absence of light, gloomy, a period of stagnation or decline.**

Against spiritual hosts of **wickedness** in the heavenly places.
Wickedness; **evil, sinful, vile, harmful, dangerous.**

Therefore take up the whole **armor** of God, that you may be able to withstand in the **evil** day, and having done all, to stand.
Armor; **Protective covering.**
Evil; **distress or wicked, causing or threatening distress or harm. A source of sorrow, calamity.**

Stand therefore, having **girded** your waist with **truth,**
Girded; **encircle or fasten (as a sword) as if with a belt. To invest with power or authority. Prepare, Brace.**

Truth; **steadfast, loyal, agreeing with facts. Consistent, honesty.**

Having put on the **breastplate** of **righteousness,**
Breastplate; **a metal plate of armor for the front part of the body between the neck and the abdomen.**
Righteousness; **virtuous, noble, moral, ethical, leaving what is just honorable, and free from guilt or wrong.**

And having shod your feet with the preparation of the **gospel** of **peace;**
Gospel; **Message, the teaching of Christ and the apostles. Accepted as infallible truth.**
Peace; **a state of calm and quiet. Freedom from disturbing thoughts or emotions.**

Above all, taking the **shield** of **faith**
Shield; **a broad piece of defensive armor carried on the arm.**
Faith; **belief and trust in God.**

With which you will be able to **quench** all the fiery **darts** of the wicked one.
Quench; **put out, extinguish.**
Darts; **something causing a sudden pain.**

And take the **helmet** of **salvation,**
Helmet; **a protective covering for the head.**

Salvation; **the saving of a person from sin or its consequences, eternal life.**

And the **sword** of the **Spirit,** which is the word of God; Sword; **a weapon with the long blade for cutting or thrusting.**
Spirit; **Holy Spirit.**

Prepare for all battles by putting on the whole Armor of God! Claim victory over satan! Stand firm! Know your position in Christ! We have His authority and power in us! Let God control your life! Walk in the light of Jesus, not darkness!

Put on the Belt of Truth! Stand firm in the truth of God's Word! Don't fall victim to satan's lies!

Put on the Breastplate of Righteousness to guard your hearts! We have protection under the blood of Jesus!

Put on the Shoes of Peace! Stand on God's Word! Shine bright for Jesus!

Put on the Shield of Faith! Destroy temptation, doubt, and all satan's fiery darts! Put on Gods shield of protection! Believe and trust Him!

Put on the Helmet of Salvation! Focus on Jesus, taking every thought captive to Jesus Christ! Leave no openings for satan!

Take the Sword of the Spirit! Prepare His Word in your heart, mind and spirit! Stand ready and powerful to expose and defeat satan!

Stand Firm in God's Army! Victory is in Jesus!

We read the Bible to arm ourselves for battle. Wisdom, knowledge and understanding of His Word gives us victory. The bible prepares us for life's journey. Everything we want to know about, marriage, children, family, business, goals, career and life is in the Bible!

Read Ephesians 6:10-19. Speak it out loud! Believe it! Place the armor of God on you! A soldier in the United States armed forces does not go into battle without protective gear. Don't forget yours!

Thank you to the brave men and woman in our military! I thank you for your protection and extraordinary service to our great country. Thank you for keeping us safe until Jesus comes to take us home with Him! God bless you!

Moses Sole Fish

Thank you Jesus! I asked you to show me how to explain the power and authority You have given us. I received my answer through the Moses Sole Fish. It reminded me of this verse,

Matthew 7:7-8 (NKJV) Ask, and it will be given to you; seek, and you will find; knock, and it will be opened to you. For everyone who asks receives, and he who seeks finds, and to him who knocks it will be opened.

Psalm 31:14 (NKJV) But as for me, I trust in You, O Lord; say, "You are my God."

II Timothy1:7 For God hath not given us the spirit of fear; but of power, and of love, and of a sound mind.

Jesus, You give us the answers in the Bible for the questions we haven't even thought of yet! Your Holy Spirit dwells in us! Through the Moses Sole, a little fish who lives in the Red Sea, You have shown the Holy Spirit power and authority we can have through Your word!

Put on the Lord Jesus Christ!

Faith Like Noah

Chapter 7

God told Noah to build the ark. He had faith and obeyed! Would we have asked, God are you serious? Rain, what rain? How big? How in the world am I going to do that?

Genesis 6:8-9 But Noah found grace in the eyes of the Lord. These are the generations of Noah: Noah was a just man and perfect in his generations, and Noah walked with God!

Noah walked with God. He was a history maker, a believer, a person who got out of the boat, even before there was water to walk on. Noah built his own boat and followed God's blueprint.

The following is a description of the ark dimensions found in the DVD by Dr. Terry Mortenson, "Noah's Flood Washing Away Millions of Years."

1 ½ Football field long
2/3 Football field wide
4 Stories high
560 Railroad cars would have fit inside the ark

Faith Like Noah

Dr. Mortenson calculated the maximum number of species on the ark. He estimated the total number of animals would not have exceeded fifty thousand.

Noah's life and the description of the ark are found in Genesis chapters 6-9. He lived to be 950 years old. It took Noah 120 years to build the ark.

There is a walkway above the street from the parking garage to the condo of my high rise building. Workers have bucket trucks to lift them up to clean the windows of the walkway. It is only 17 feet high. Noah had to go up four stories. He did not have a fork lift, elevator or crane. He did not have power tools or other modern day equipment. He had only his children to help. It was much more than asking them to do basic tasks.

For 120 years, his family was committed to Noah. They worked side by side. Noah must have had a wonderful relationship with his family. Do you think they ate meals together? Prayed together? Do you pray with your children?

In this fast paced, fast food world, do you take time to eat a meal together as a family? Maybe you are not building an ark, but you can spend quality time. Work as a family on a project. Clean out the garage. Wash the car. Work is easier when we do it together!

Faith Like Noah

Don't let your family grow apart. We can also grow apart from God. We may think we have been away too long, drifted too far or made too many mistakes. Jesus loves us! He always forgives and welcomes us with open arms.

I believe Noah spoke words of faith, encouragement and love over his family. How many times did he tell his family he loved them? How often did he give them a hug or say great job? How many times did he tell his family how proud he was of them? How often did he climb to the top of the ark and in the presence of God kneel in prayer? God found Noah perfect and they walked together.

Do you think he had family issues similar to ours? Did he say, Lord, I had an argument with my son today, please forgive me? Give me wisdom to mend my relationship with him. Did he pray, God, I'm so tired, I need your strength? Was his prayer, what are Your instructions? I believe he may have said, God, I have peace in Your presence! Keep me on course! I praise Your name!

This is not about Noah's life. It is about you and your family. Where you are with God or where you can be with God. Noah had a blueprint for the ark. God has a blueprint for your life. It is spectacular!

Faith Like Noah

Noah lived to age 950, more than ten times longer than our average life span. Could we do something that would take us twenty years if God asked? Would it be too overwhelming?

Noah walked with Jesus! He had faith! Walk with Jesus and have that same kind of faith! Wake in the morning and say, "Good morning Jesus, where are we headed today? I'm available, make me usable!" Take your walk with Jesus one step and one day at a time. He will teach you! Have faith! We need to be like Noah!

Can you imagine what it must have been like for Noah and his family when they first saw dry land. Imagine how they felt when they landed. Now there was a "boat to step out of!" Noah had great faith and trusted in God!

"Faith sees the invisible, believes the unbelievable, and receives the impossible." Corrie Ten Boom (A Dutch Christian who helped many Jews escape the Nazi Holocaust).

Romans 12:3 (NKJV) For I say, through the grace given to me, to everyone who is among you, not to think of himself more highly than he ought to think, but to think soberly, as God has dealt to each one a measure of faith.

Faith Like Noah

God's word says we all receive a measure of faith. So why does it seem some people have more? They trust in God, believe and do not doubt. We can do the same!

Faith like Noah, reminds me of the renowned Christian artist Carman. His career started in the 1980's. He is an evangelist, singer, songwriter, television/film actor and author with numerous accolades including several Dove Awards. Carman has sold over ten million records. He has 15 platinum CDs and videos. Carman's accomplishments are detailed on his website **carman.org**.

Carman is a man who never stops standing up for God! He knows we are here to win souls for Jesus! Carman has many talents and abilities, but his greatest love is being sold out for the Lord! Carman has served Him since the beginning of his salvation. Carman had the largest Christian concert in history! He has led over one million people to Christ!

February 14, 2013, Valentine's Day, Carman was diagnosed with cancer. His doctor told him he had only five years to live. Some of his close relatives and siblings did not call him. The lady he believed he might marry did not think she could walk the journey with him. Heartbreaking! Carman posted his health condition on Facebook. His Facebook exploded with thousands of loving messages, encouraging words and prayers for God's healing!

In an announcement, Carman promised he would record a new CD and video. Additionally, he would embark on his first national tour in 14 years. The tour would take him to 100 stages across the USA!

The next eight months, Carman was deep in chemo and fighting for his life. He finished recording the CD and the video screens for his tour while in treatment. Weeks after being released, Carman started the tour.

He had little energy and struggled to get through each show. It was hard to do the meet and greets that followed each concert. Carman did them all! By the end of each concert, he was exhausted. He would return to his bus and "crash" for twelve hours. Now, Carman is healthy and strong. He works out at the gym. He really crushed the devil under his feet! As of December 2014, Carman was 48 concerts away from fulfilling his promise! He has won 2500 more souls for Jesus!

His CD is titled "No Plan B!" It contains a variety of beautiful songs including Jesus Heal Me, Peace of the Lord, I Did My Best. I really love the message in his songs. Here are a few lines from the title track, No Plan B. "The road's been a long one, it's always been a fight. Gods had my back. He's been my plan "A!"

Living for the Lord and No Plan B!" Carman is on God's path! He serves Jesus! God bless you Carman!

God has a path, a plan for each of us. It is not Carman's, Noah's or my plan. God has a plan for you!

Jeremiah 29:11-13 (NKJV) For I know the thoughts that I think toward you, says the Lord, thoughts of peace and not of evil, to give you a future and hope. Then you will call upon Me and go and pray to Me, and I will listen to you. And will seek Me and find Me, when you search for Me with all your heart.

Pray and talk with God. Ask Him, "Where are you leading me? I want to follow your plan for my life." Know your Bible as well as you know the way around your home. Memorize scriptures so you are always prepared. One of my favorites:

Luke 1:37 For with God nothing shall be impossible!

Pay attention to what God is telling you! Listen for His voice. Pray, "God, I believe You are telling me this. Confirm it for me or close the door if I'm headed in the wrong direction."

Faith Like Noah

Sometimes we limit ourselves. We don't think we are qualified for the job He wants us to do. When God revealed I was supposed to write this book, I started telling my friends. I was speaking it into existence.

I was in class one day at Charis Bible College. My teacher, Pastor Greg stopped his lesson and spoke a God word over me. Part of what he said was a confirmation for me to write this book!

School was going to be over in about a month. Time to make it happen! God said He would go before. He guides my path. I prayed for His wisdom. I ask for His knowledge and understanding to write and publish this book. God helps us! We need to move forward and complete our journey.

James 1:5 (NKJV) If any of you lacks wisdom, let him ask of God, Who gives to all liberally and without reproach, and it will be given to him.

Remember, God is The Potter, we are the clay. I am amazed how He has expanded my horizons. I have become a minister, author and now God has me writing music! How wonderful and completely unique are we, when our faith gives Jesus permission to shape and mold our lives. I want my life to be Holy Spirit inspired! I want to have more faith than Noah, an "Abundance!"

Prayer Parts Water

Chapter 8

Isaiah 43:16 Thus saith the Lord, which maketh a way in the sea, and a path in the mighty waters.

Isaiah 58:11 (NKJV) The Lord will guide you continually, And satisfy your soul in drought, And strengthen your bones; you shall be like a watered garden, And like a spring of water, whose waters do not fail.

Psalm 55:17 Evening and, morning, and at noon, will I pray, and cry aloud: and He shall hear my voice.

Mark 11:23-24 For verily I say unto you, That whosoever shall say unto this mountain, be thou removed, and be thou cast into the sea; and shall not doubt in his heart, but shall believe that those things which he saith shall come to pass; he shall have whatsoever he saith. Therefore I say unto you, what things soever you desire, when you pray believe that you receive them, and ye shall have them.

"Prayer is simply a two way conversation between you and God."

- Billy Graham

Have you ever noticed several scriptures are repeated in the Bible? We need to pay attention! When God tells us something more than once, it is important. We repeat things to our children. We want them to remember our words as they grow up! We want our important teachings to stay with them. God wants the same! Read His word daily!

Proverb 22:6 Train up a child in the way he should go: and when he is old, he will not depart from it.

Do you have someone to pray with? A prayer buddy? If you do not, pray for a prayer partner to come into your life. Ask for a person you can trust. One who has faith to move mountains. A pray warrior who doesn't doubt or waiver.

How do I find a person like that? Pray a prayer like this, "Dear Heavenly Father, touch my heart, soul, and spirit right now. I want to know You in a personal relationship. Anything that is not from the Holy Spirit in me needs to leave now in the name of Jesus. Break off my negative ways and words. Overflow me with

Your wisdom, knowledge and understanding. Jesus, give my heart a fire and passion for You and Your word. Your word is a lamp onto my feet to guide my path. Lord, make it a huge flood light so I stay on the right path with You! Cover me in the blood of Jesus. Send Your angels to stand guard over me. Lord, I ask in Your name, send a person to pray with. Put their name in my spirit. Put them in my path! Thank you Heavenly Father for the person You are placing in my life to pray with!"

Jesus always answers our prayers. Pray for your prayer partner, even if you do not yet know who they are. Listen for God's voice. He may tell you to go somewhere such as a church event or social gathering to bring you together. We pray! We believe! We receive! We praise and thank Him!

We may not see the answer right away. We need to trust and believe God. There are no unanswered prayers (Daniel 9 & 10).

It is like when a trusted friend says they are going to do something. Someone else says, "They won't do that." We know if our friend says it will happen, it will! We know in our heart they won't let us down. God's word does not return void!

Isaiah 55:11 So shall My word be that goeth forth out of My mouth: it shall not return unto Me void, but it shall accomplish that which I please,and it shall prosper in the thing whereto I sent it.

I received a business flier at my condo for a sound studio. I kept the flier and stopped in to ask a few music related questions. I met the owners, Pamela and her husband Stephen. Their studio sound set is fully equipped. They also offer voice and music lessons. They enjoy helping people on their music journey. Five minutes into the conversation, I felt a divine connection from God. It felt I had known Pamela a very long time. When we know Jesus, we are one in His Spirit! Pamela and I ended up not only discussing music questions but audio for this book! This was the first time I thought about an audio version.

Later, Pamela and I met for lunch. She told me she and her husband had moved to Florida two years ago. She said, "I have been praying for a friend. One who knows Jesus and His power and love." A prayer, a flier, conversation and fellowship. It is an example of how our God works! Pamela is a very talented, amazing woman of God! She told me, "We pray over our business before we start the day!" I love that!

Prayer Parts Water

We can also pray with someone over the phone. My niece Kimberly is a blessing and a prayer warrior. We pray in the morning before she starts work. She arrives at her job 45 minutes early so we have time to pray. It is dark on the road in the morning. She waits until she is safely at work. Then Monday through Friday we pray together by phone.

Sometimes life gets in the way of prayer. We cannot let it! Prayer and reading God's word are as important as putting on our clothes! Make time to pray to God, by yourself or with someone.

Kimberly and I pray about all things. She recently said, "I always believed in prayer. Together, it seems we are moving mountains!" Pray with others and stand in agreement for requests to our Heavenly Father!

Matthew 18:19-20 Again I say unto you, That if two of you shall agree on earth as touching anything that they shall ask, it shall be done for them of My Father which is in Heaven. For where two or three are gathered together in My Name, there am I in the midst of them.

Kimberly and I prayed for her husband Jay to start exercising. We praised God every day for Jay getting in shape. We prayed Jay would have a passion to exercise. We thought he would join our fitness club. Instead, God put YMCA swimming in our spirit. It is an activity for the whole family. Jay was overweight. Swimming at the YMCA was the perfect start for him. The first month it seemed every muscle in his body ached. Swimming laps, Jay was using muscles he had neglected.

My brother Craig is Kimberly's dad. He also joined and helped encourage Jay. In a short time, Jay found himself sleeping and feeling better. Now he says, "I love swimming!" We are so proud of him! He got out of the boat and swam! Stepping out and getting started is not easy. God answered our prayer!

Do you ever wake up in the early morning hours and wonder why? It may be God's alarm clock. Is there something He wants us to know? Is He giving us an answer to a prayer? Does He want us to pray for someone? A name or face may come in our spirit.

If you are not sure how to pray, just start! You can begin like this, "Lord help me, how should I pray? Give me wisdom, knowledge and understanding." When we step out in faith, God will give us the words we need through His Spirit. Step out of the boat and follow Him. Jesus is the one that shows us how to walk on water and beyond!

I Thessalonians 5:17 Pray without ceasing.

Prayer parts water! Don't let prayer be absent from your life. Let prayer be non-stop in your spirit! Help me Jesus! He knows our problem and **He is the answer.**

Psalm 121:2 My help cometh from the Lord, which made heaven and earth.

We need to seek Him! Ask Jesus!

Matthew 7:7-8 Ask, and it shall be given you; seek and ye shall find; knock and it shall be opened unto you; For everyone that asketh receiveth; and he that seeketh findeth; and to him that knocketh it shall be opened.

Our Father knows what it is we need before we ask Him. His word says to search the scriptures daily. Pray!

Ask in Jesus name!

John 14:13-16 And whatsoever ye shall ask in My name, that will I do, that the Father may be glorified in the Son. If yea shall ask anything in My name, I will do it. If you love Me, keep My commandments. And I will pray the Father, and He shall give you

another Comforter, that He may abide with you forever.

Colossians 3:17 And whatsoever ye do in word or deed, do all in the name of the Lord Jesus, giving thanks to God and the Father by Him.

Matthew 21:22 And all things, whatsoever he shall ask in prayer, believing ye shall receive.

God's word also tells us to humble ourselves and pray! Seek His face! Pray always!

Philippians 4:6-7 Be careful for nothing, but in everything by prayer and supplication with thanksgiving let your requests be known unto God. And the peace of God which passes all understanding, shall keep your hearts and your minds through Christ Jesus.

Give praise and thanksgiving to God even before we receive the evidence of the answer for our prayer. Praise Him! Thank Him! Speak your prayer into existence!

Some of my family wanted to come to Florida over the Christmas season. They were going to drive from Minnesota in two vehicles. There were three adults and nine children traveling. It was too expensive to fly.

Prayer Parts Water

Kimberly, other family members and I started praying together in September about the trip. We asked God to go before and provide the time off work, affordable gas prices, good weather conditions and safe travels. We prayed for the understanding of family members who would not be able to make the trip. Then our prayers were of thanksgiving and praise to Jesus even before we knew the outcome.

Kimberly's husband Jay has a job that would not allow him to be off work during Christmas and New Year's week. He sacrificed being with his family so they could see the ocean for the first time and enjoy warm weather and fun! I thank Jay for his generous heart and understanding!

It was a twenty hour trip each way. The weather was great. Both vehicles ran well. The drive time seemed to fly by for them. The children were well behaved. Now that's a miracle!

When we started praying, gas prices were high. November 2014, gas prices started coming down. By the time my family traveled, prices were under two dollars a gallon in some places along their route. The gas prices dropped almost in half! Did we think it was luck? No, that was an answered prayer! It was God! I don't believe in luck. I believe in God! He is a sure thing

One day the kids were in the ocean. It was cloudy to the right and left of us. The sun was shining and the sky was clear in front of my condo where they were swimming! Did we think it was luck? No, that was God! Praise God! We don't take His goodness and mercy for granted!

The beautiful sunshine sparkled on the water before us. The love of God that reaches to the Heavens! His faithfulness encompasses the skies! I want to greet the Son of God each morning! I want to walk with Him. I want to taste and see He is good!

Lamentations 3:22-23 It is the Lord's mercies that we are not consumed, because His compassion fail not. They are new every morning, Great is Thy faithfulness.

II Corinthians 5:7 For we walk by faith, not by sight.

Psalm 34:8 O taste and see that the Lord is good: blessed is the man that trusteth in Him.

We become more valuable employees at work through learning, training and experience. We learn to anticipate, prevent and correct problems. Our job becomes easier as we attain more knowledge and understanding. We can rise to new positions in the company.

God wants His very best for us! We must seek Him, know His Word. The Bible is a fountain of knowledge! His Word helps us prevent, correct and solve problems. I've learned to stay close, how to pray and use the Bible as my manual and best tool! The answers are all in the Bible! Pray! Stay close to God!

John 14:26 But the Comforter, which is the Holy Ghost, whom the Father will send in My name, He shall teach you all things, and bring all things to your remembrance, whatsoever I have said unto you.

Teach us all things and bring all things to our remembrance. This also applies to what we want to remember for our jobs etc. When our children study for a test and want to remember what they learn, they can call on their Heavenly Father for help. It is very powerful when we pray and attach a scripture. God's Word does not return void!

God wants us healthy!

III John 1:2 Beloved, I wish above all things that thou may prosper and be in health, even as thy soul prospereth.

God wants us to have prosperity.

Psalm 35:27 Let them shout for joy, and be glad, that favor My righteous cause, yea, let them say continually, Let the Lord be magnified which has pleasure in the prosperity of His servant.

God wants to give us the desires of our heart.

Psalm 37:4 Delight thyself also in the Lord; and He shall give thee the desires of thine heart.

Trust Him.

Psalm 37:5 Commit thy way unto the Lord; trust also in Him; He shall bring it to pass.

Order my steps Lord.

Psalm 37:23 The steps of a good man are ordered by the Lord: and He delighteth in his way.

Give the battle to the Lord.

Psalm 35:1-2 Plead my cause, O Lord, with them that strive with me: fight against them that fight against me. Take hold of shield and buckler, and stand up for mine help.

Pray!

Psalm 5:1-3 Give ear to my words, O Lord, consider my meditation. Hearken unto my voice of my cry, my King, and my God: for unto Thee will I pray. My voice shalt Thou hear in the morning, O Lord; in the morning will I direct my prayers unto Thee, and will look up.

Trust!

Psalm 18:30 As for God, His way is perfect: the word of the Lord is tried: He is a buckler to all those that trust in Him.
Great is the Lord!

Praise!

Psalm 113:3 From the rising of the sun unto the going down of the same the Lord's name is to be praised.

Prayer Parts Water

In Minnesota, we prepare for winter road conditions. We have extra warm clothes and blankets. We put bags of sand and salt in the trunk of our cars in case we get stuck in the snow. We have a shovel and a scraper at the ready to remove snow and ice from our vehicle. When I'm prepared, I usually don't get stuck in the snow.

God wants us to be wise and prepared. Jesus loves us! He wants us safe in Him. Everything we want to know about life, business, career, marriage, friends, etc. is in the Bible! We need to ask our Heavenly Father for instructions found in His word and through prayer. Attend and get involved in a church. Learn! Grow! Worship Jesus!

I look forward to Heaven! I especially love the part of the Lord's Prayer, "On earth as it is in Heaven." I believe God gives us heaven on earth days, everyday! We need to recognize when the devil comes against us and give the battle to God! Trust Him! Thank and praise Him! The devil wants us to lose our peace. God will keep us in His perfect peace if we keep our minds focused on Him! God is so good all the time. We need to receive all He has for us. He wants to bless us!

I was serving as a prayer minister at a Christian concert. Before the music started, one of the girls said, " I had a dream last night. I was going up to Heaven on an escalator with other people also on it. There was another down escalator going towards hell. There were people on it that I knew. They said to me, you knew Jesus and you never told us about Him."

We have the responsibility to share Jesus to give others an opportunity to receive Him into their heart. We must give the Holy Spirit permission to use us. We have the boldness of Christ when we allow Him to make us usable!

Acts 4:31 (NKJV) And when they had prayed, the place where they were assembled together was shaken, and they were all filled with the Holy Spirit, and they spoke the word of God with boldness!

"Prayer should be the key of the day and the lock of the night."

- George Herbert

Romans 12:12 (NKJV) Rejoicing in hope, patient in tribulation, continuing steadfastly in prayer.

The Lord's Prayer, Matthew 6:9-13 After this manner therefore pray ye; Our Father which art in Heaven. Hallowed be Thy name. Thy Kingdom come. Thy will be done in earth, as it is in Heaven. Give us this day our daily bread. And forgive us our debts, as we forgive our debtors. And lead us not into temptation, but deliver us from evil: For Thine is the Kingdom, and the power, and the glory, forever. AMEN

Let the Healing Begin

Chapter 9

Does God Heal? The Bible says He heals **all** manner of sickness and disease. There are many verses in the Bible for healing:

Matthew 4:23   And Jesus went about all Galilee, teaching in their synagogues preaching the gospel of the kingdom, and healing all manner of sickness and all manner of disease among people.

Matthew 10:1 And when He had called unto Him His twelve disciples, He gave them power against unclean spirits to cast them out and to heal all manner of sickness and all manner of disease.

Does God sometimes give us sickness to teach us a lesson? **No!** He took all sickness and disease! **By His stripes we are healed!**

Let the Healing Begin

Isaiah 53:5 But He was wounded for our transgressions, He was bruised for our iniquities: the chastisement of our peace was upon Him and with His stripes we are healed.

He took, not gave it. He didn't say going to be healed! We are healed! Jesus died on the cross for our sins. By His stripes we are healed! Jesus was ridiculed, beaten and tortured. He had a crown of thorns embedded into His head. He was forced to carry a heavy wooden cross. Nails were driven through His hands and feet. At any time, He could have spoken to His Heavenly Father and it would have stopped. Jesus knew the gift He was giving us. All we have to do is **receive it!**

Sickness and healing! Two words that change our lives! God wants us physically and emotionally well! My beautiful daughter Kelly, was born with cystic fibrosis, a disease of the lungs. Doctors say it is an incurable disease, but I always believed God would heal her. Kelly did really well for a long time. She held her lung capacity at 60% for several years.

When Kelly was 29 years old she had to change doctors. Up until then, she had a pediatric doctor and went to Children's Hospital. Kelly should have had to change doctors years before.

Let the Healing Begin

The next two years setbacks occurred. Kelly's health was failing. The last year of her life she also had vertigo. It caused dizziness. The room seemed to be constantly spinning. Kelly had to be heavily sedated in order to sleep.

Kelly's brother Ryan was seven years her junior. Despite the difference in age, they were close. A child with an illness requires more of a parent's time. I always tried to balance my love and affection. At times more attention had to be focused on Kelly because of her condition.

Ryan was a talented child, gifted in whatever he put his mind to do. For instance, he learned to play the harmonica and guitar. He mastered the music scales and started playing songs. Much of what he learned was self-taught. Whether it was rollerblading down hills, riding a unicycle in the entire Fourth of July parade as Uncle Sam, performing magic acts, juggling or break dancing, Ryan was and still is a natural!

My beautiful children spent a lot of time together. They shared many great moments and would laugh and laugh! Ryan would change his voice to imitate someone else like a celebrity and go into a hilarious routine. The two of them would watch a program on TV that seemed a waste of time to me. They would roll on the floor laughing. It would make Kelly cough uncontrollably and I would have to make them stop.

Even in later years, Ryan and Kelly would act like kids again whenever they got together. Like most brothers and sisters, there were times they did not get along. They always had each other's back and shared a special bond of love. The laughter and happy times were great medicine not just for Kelly, but for all of us!

Kelly was in and out of the hospital many times. The support of my family and friends was awesome! They would visit Kelly. They brought fun surprises including balloons, flowers, candy and an assortment of gifts to encourage and lift her spirits. When she was older, I did not have to be at the hospital 24/7 during Kelly's stays. I got a break with help from my friends who came to see her.

Why is visiting the hospital so exhausting? Is there something in the air or is it the uncomfortable chairs in the room? There are family gathering areas down the hall. Sick patients and visitors share the same chairs. There is the question of germs and infection. Seems like a good way to start as a visitor and end up a patient. It was better to sit in the uncomfortable chairs in Kelly's room.

Let the Healing Begin

I always tried to keep Kelly's spirit upbeat. She was in the hospital a lot for what the doctors called a "tune up." It was similar to checking and adjusting a car engine, except in this case it was Kelly's lungs.

I remember one year in December, her condition worsened. Kelly's doctor admitted her. He told me she would probably have to stay four to six weeks. This meant she would be in the hospital on Christmas!

At that point, I wanted to keep her mind off Christmas. I said, "Let's have a '50's party!" I got some fun posters to decorate her room. I set the date, called friends and family and invited them to the party. I asked them to wear '50's attire.

The day of the party, I brought in a crock pot with sloppy joe's, buns, chips, dessert and ice cold root beer in bottles. One of the nurses mistook the root beer for bottles of regular beer. She assumed we were drinking alcohol. The nurse came into the room visibly upset until she realized the bottles were soda not beer. She never mentioned anything about the music and dancing.

My friend Jane arrived in the room wearing a hospital gown. It was the kind that is wide open in back with only two ties. She put it on over her clothes and marched in portraying herself as a doctor. She started carrying on and told Kelly, "You will be as good as new and chasing those cute doctors down the hall!" It was such a fun time! Some of the nurses came in and joined us for sloppy joe's and dessert. Eventually they had to shut us down. Laughter and joy had filled the room! There were no thoughts of sickness!

Proverb 17:22 A merry heart doeth good like a medicine: but a broken spirit drieth the bones.

I almost want to cry thinking about how wonderful my family and friends are. They dropped what they were doing in the busiest month of the year to come for Kelly. This hospital is located near downtown Minneapolis. The drive in the winter weather varied from thirty minutes to an hour each way. My friends and family are a blessing from heaven! Thank you!

It was nearing Christmas. Kelly was still in the hospital. The time came to decorate her room! I draped lights around the bottom of her bed and ran a cord under the bed to the headboard. I put Christmas decorations in her windows that lit up. With all the bright hospital lights off, Christmas music playing on low and just the Christmas lights on, it did not have the feel of a hospital room. It was great until the fire marshal showed up. In the spirit of Christmas, he allowed the decorations to remain. We just couldn't have the lights on.

Let the Healing Begin

Kelly had a china doll complexion. Her laugh was infectious. Those who met her loved her. Purple was her favorite color. She liked everything mint. Mint smells, mint flavors, mint tea, mint chocolates!

She would talk about something that happened. She made the story come alive! It felt like you had been there too! I always thought Kelly should be a doctor. At times, she seemed to know as much as they did! Kelly received her computer from my parents. She used it to witness to people all over the world, especially kids with cystic fibrosis.

Kelly and I knew God heals! We thought it had to be a minister or someone laying hands on her. Certainly, it would require a person more powerful then us. After all, this was big! An incurable disease! We searched out ministers for healing. We needed to look to the Healer Himself, Jesus!

When Kelly went to heaven I remember praying and asking God, "Was I not specific in my prayers? I wanted her healed on earth." I knew she would be healed in heaven! My heart broke in a million pieces! I had a memorial service on a Monday night so all her friends could attend.

When the service was over, my mother asked if I wanted to come to her home. I declined. I wanted to be alone and talk to God. I got into my car and headed for the freeway. It was about 10:30 at night and pitch dark. Suddenly, the heavens opened up into many exquisite colors! The brilliance of God's glory surrounded me! It was like the most beautiful sunrise and sunset had combined and encompassed the entire sky. How do I describe what I had never seen before? It was a sight greater than I could imagine! Like a glimpse of Heaven!

It was a thirty minute drive home. It felt like I was there in the blink of an eye. I thought about the words my daughter had spoken to me, "When I get to heaven, I will give you a really big sign!" I had told her, "I don't need a sign. I know you're going to heaven Kelly!"

The first time I asked God to show me everything about healing was after Kelly died. Why didn't I ask sooner? What was I thinking? Anyone that has lost someone close knows it is hard to move on. There were months it seemed I cried all night. In the morning, I put on the face everyone wanted to see and went to work. I wore a smile and when anyone asked me if I was OK, I lied.

The Bible tells us the enemy comes to kill, steal and destroy (John 10:10). I felt the devil was trying to destroy me. Does the enemy know God's plans for us? It seems he works overtime to stop us! He knows how much Jesus loves us! I felt so low! I thought if I just stayed in bed and did not eat, maybe I would go to heaven too. I cannot believe those thoughts entered my head. Me who is always positive plus!

God gave me Ryan. He knew I would need him. My son was strong for me and God said, "Your son needs you Laura." As tears rolled down my face, all I could say was, "Help me Jesus!" It was a long road. The journey became easier the more I learned.

I was attending Hosanna church. I started going to a class called "Water of Life." It was a nine week discipleship course, one night a week. A variety of topics on emotional life changing healings are taught. The class on words seemed to be directed at me. I needed to change the words I spoke over myself.

We get up in the morning and sometimes say things about ourselves without thinking. My back hurts. I can't stand work. I bet my boss is going to give me the worst job. We say things about our spouse, friends, family, etc. Do not talk negatively. We need to speak positive words over our life for what we want. We will see a change in how we feel! Others will see it in us!

Start each day by saying, "Good morning Jesus! Wow, it's a beautiful day! What do you have for us? I feel ready to part the waters, move the mountains! Thank You Heavenly Father for my Holy Spirit energy and my Holy Spirit youth! Thank You for my perfect healthy body in Christ! Thank You for Your angels that stand guard over me, my home and family! Raise me up to accomplish the plans You have for me. I love You Jesus!"

The journey became lighter as I learned more. He was emotionally healing me. Hurdles became easier. God never said life would be easy. He did say In Isaiah 54:17 no weapon formed against us would prosper. He would never leave us.

Jesus will walk with us in the valley, carry us if needed. My emotional healing continued. I started watching Andrew Wommack on television. Andrew spoke on many topics from the Bible. I also enjoyed reading his books on healing including, "God Wants You Well" and "You've Already Got It." I learned more and more about healing.

I was working at a new construction model home. The garage was converted into a Welcome Center with glass doors. On the side of each door was a large planter pot. An evergreen tree was planted in each for the

Christmas season. I managed to find the one patch of ice just outside the door. My feet came out from under me. I did not have time to say or do anything, but in my mind I prayed, help me Jesus! I say that a lot. My left elbow came down in the dirt of the planter. My ribs hit the edge of the planter and took most of the impact.

I had my phone but did not call for help. I said out loud, "I'm going to be okay! I'm all right! Thank You Jesus!" I slid myself along the pavement until I was off the ice. I walked into my office holding my left arm close to my body. I called my manager to see if I had to turn in a report. She said to go to the doctor and get approved to return to work.

I kept speaking to my pain telling it to get out in the name of Jesus. Getting into my car was almost unbearable, but I drove myself to the clinic. The doctor came into the room to examine me. She asked me to breathe in and out. The pain felt like childbirth, but I did not acknowledge it.

The doctor advised me she needed to take x-rays because of work comp requirements. She did not think my ribs were broken. The doctor was surprised when the x rays revealed I had two cracked ribs.

Keep in mind, I had shown no sign of my pain to her. The doctor said, "Laura, you are going to be in excruciating pain for seven or eight weeks." I said, "You know me Doctor, I'm a woman of faith." The doctor said the only thing she could do for broken ribs was give me pain pills.

The doctor did not think I had cracked ribs until she saw the x-ray. I had spoken to my pain and cast it out in the name of Jesus. I stood on God's words! By His stripes I'm healed! I continued to thank and praise Jesus for my healing.

I went back to work in four days. It took two weeks for the pain to leave completely. That was far less than the seven or eight weeks the doctor had indicated! My attitude is the devil will not steal anything from me! I believe if the doctor does not know of my pain, the devil doesn't either. Unless I tell him! I speak out the words I want over my life! I have the power and authority in Jesus!

Romans 4:17.......and calleth those things which be not as though they were.

I know God heals! I was not going to let anything block my healing. When I spoke the words of healing over my body, what was the delay? Knowing what I now know, I would have said, "I don't receive the words spoken by the doctor." I should have broken off the doctor's words of excruciating pain in the name of Jesus.

The devil knew it was my first attempt at healing. God wants His people to have knowledge in all things! My injury experience built my confidence! I had prayed over myself. I looked forward to praying over others!

My friend Rudy was 87 years old. He was in the hospital suffering from lack of circulation and pain in his leg. When I arrived, he had been there almost three days. He was still in a lot of pain. The toes of his left foot were bandaged. I asked if I could take a look. He let me. All five of the toes on his left foot were very black. There was certainly reason for concern.

I began talking with Rudy. I asked, "If you were to die, do you know where you are going?" He answered, "I sure hope I'm going to heaven!" I asked, "Do you want to be sure? Do you want to ask Jesus in your heart now? Then you will know you are going to heaven when you die." He prayed and accepted Jesus into his heart that night!

Rudy's son was my boyfriend when I was 15 years old. He had passed away several years before from cancer. I told Rudy in the hospital, "Your son accepted Jesus long ago. He is in heaven!"

Rudy's wife Anna called the hospital from home. We should never assume someone is saved. I knew I needed to talk to Anna. She also accepted Jesus into her heart that night! Praise God!

Before I left, I asked Rudy if I could pray for him. I prayed over his pain and for the circulation in his leg and black toes to be healed in the name of Jesus. I called him the next day. I asked how he was doing. Rudy said, "Right after you left, my pain went away and didn't come back." I said, "Praise the Lord!" I asked, "How are your toes?" He said, "I cannot see them, they are bandaged." I told him I would not be able to get to the hospital that day, but would be there the next day after work. I told Rudy to keep thanking and praising Jesus!

I continued to praise the Lord for Rudy's lack of pain and the healing of his leg and toes. When thoughts of doubt or unbelief tried to push their way into my mind, I spoke out loud talking confidently of white toes and a healthy body. A perfect body in Christ! I praised and thanked the Lord for Rudy's healing! When we talk out loud it is hard to think about something else.

I went to the hospital the next day. The moment I arrived, I wanted to look at his toes. As I pulled back the bandages, I got a glimpse of his baby toe. It was white. My heart was pounding! I uncovered his left foot. I saw four white toes with circulation restored. His big toe was still black. Wow, thank You Jesus! Natural healing in two days would be impossible. It was a healing from God!

Psalm 30:2 O lord my God, I cried unto Thee, and Thou hast healed me.

Isaiah 58:8 Then shall thy light break forth as the morning, and thine health shall spring forth speedily: and thy righteousness shall go before thee; the glory of the Lord shall be thy reward.

Healing someone is not about us. It is allowing the Holy Spirit to use us and work through us. Remember, we are the instrument and God is the Healer. All glory goes to Jesus!

Rudy was released from the hospital and went home. A few weeks later, I talked to him on the phone. He said, "My doctor wants to cut off my left leg." I said, "We are not receiving that in the name of Jesus." His wife was on an extension phone. The three of us prayed in agreement for the healing of Rudy's leg. We praised the Lord for His healing grace!

Rudy went to the hospital the next day. The doctor did not amputate his leg. He only removed the dead skin from his big toe. Four years later, Rudy still has his leg and all his toes. Thank you Jesus!

I quit my job and moved to Colorado to attend Charis Bible College. The college also has a healing school on Thursday that is open to the public. I went through training and became a prayer minister at Charis Bible College. I was learning and absorbing, soaking in the Lord! I met a couple who were attending the college. Their daughter had been diagnosed with cystic fibrosis, the so called "incurable" disease. She was healed!

JESUS HEALS

By Natural process!
By His word!
By a miracle!
By a gift of healing!
By prayer of agreement!
By His Healing Grace!
By the faith of the sick person!

Let the Healing Begin

My friend Edna has been in the nursing field for over forty years. She observed that patients and their families always wanted doctors to name and identify their sickness. "Instead they should cast out all symptoms in the name of Jesus," she said. Stop worrying and acknowledging sickness. Start praying, believing and receiving the healing power of God! He is our Healer!

Yes, I also believe in doctors. I believe God uses doctors, but they do not have the last word. The doctor's report may say the condition is hopeless, months to live, terminal. Seek God's report! Doctors are not the authority, Jesus is. He wants us well!

I know there are several ways healing occurs. Jesus has many methods to heal. One time, He rubbed mud in a blind man's eyes. Another time, He took the person out of the city because there was so much unbelief. A woman touched the hem of Jesus's robe in faith and was healed.

Proverbs 18:21 Death and life are in the power of the tongue: and they that love it shall eat the fruit thereof.

We must pay attention to the words we speak over ourselves. For example, never say, "It is flu season, I'll probably get the flu. I say, "No, I don't receive that."

Psalm 91:10   There shall no evil befall thee, neither shall any plague come nigh thy dwelling.

No plague! We do not have to receive any plague in our home. This includes colds, flu, Ebola, all sickness and disease. Jesus already took it on the cross for us. God says His word does not return void. Seek a scripture for your need! Stand on it! Believe it! Don't doubt or waiver!

James 1:6   But let him ask in faith nothing wavering. For he that wavereth is like a wave of the sea driven with the wind and tossed.

Mark 11:23   For verily I say unto to you, That whosoever shall say unto this mountain, be thou removed, and be thou cast into the sea; and shall not doubt in his heart, but shall believe that those things which he saith shall come to pass; he shall have whatsoever he saith.

God gave us the same authority as Jesus to speak to our mountain. For example, my arm hurts. I speak to it, "Pain in my arm, I cast you out in the name of Jesus. I speak words of health and healing in my body." Should it leave right then? Yes! If not, I say again, "Pain get out in the name of Jesus, you have no authority over me."

No matter how my body feels, I praise and thank the Lord for my healing. I follow in faith, not by how I feel. I speak these words of health over my body, "Thank You for the perfect body of Christ in me. Thank You Lord, for taking all sickness and disease on the cross for me. Thank You Lord, for my Holy Spirit health. Thank You Lord, for all Your blessings and favor. Cover me in the Blood of Jesus."

We can also pray for others. Ask Jesus how to pray for their healing. There may be a root cause. One night I was with five of my girlfriends. We were having dinner at one of their homes. One of the girls asked us to pray before we ate. She said her whole body was in pain.

We gathered around her. I sat next to her and put my hand on her knee. I heard the prayers of the others. I would have prayed similarly, except I first asked God, "How should I pray for her?" He gave me a question to ask my friend. When I did she answered, "I'm in fear of losing my job. I recently lost my mother."

God showed me the root. It was fear, loneliness and anxiety. I had my friend speak those words out and break them off in the name of Jesus. I asked her to be refilled with God's overflowing love, joy and peace. My friends changed the prayers they were speaking over her. Within minutes, her pain was gone. Praise God! We have to ask the Holy Spirit for His knowledge and wisdom on all things.

Mark 11:25-26 (NKJV) And whenever you stand praying, if you have anything against anyone, forgive him, that Your Father in Heaven may also forgive you your trespasses. "But if you do not forgive, neither will Your Father in Heaven forgive your trespasses."

There is another road block to healing. It is unforgiveness. Remember, God says forgive or He does not forgive us. Keep in mind, we are forgiving them, not the action itself. The story of Joseph is a good example. (Genesis 37-50) Joseph's brothers left him for dead. Over several years, Joseph rose to a position of importance. There was a famine. His brothers came for food. They thought he was dead. The relationship was restored, but Joseph held his brothers at a distance. Sometimes, we cannot give trust back.

Lord, by your stripes I'm **healed**!

Let the Healing Begin

I stand on His Word!
I'm committed to **healing**!
I'm **healed** because He said so!
Pray to the Father in the Name of Jesus!
Healed because of the Word not how I feel!
God's **healing** power is in me!
Healing is part of the kingdom!
My heart is fixed on trusting Jesus!
God wants me well!
His Word is **healing**!

We need to be confident in healing! Someone asks, "Are you sick?" Do not keep talking about what is wrong with you. Stop speaking sickness. Jesus took your sickness on the cross. Start speaking words of wellness! Speak words of healing such as, "I'm fighting something off, I'm walking in victory. I can do all things in Christ who strengthens me. I speak blessings over my body. God wants me well! Father, I thank you that healing has already been done. I lay hold of it with my faith! I believe! I receive! By your stripes I'm healed!"

If you have just started reading the Bible, begin with Psalms and Proverbs. Then go to the New Testament. Read a verse and speak the words into your life. For example, you want more joy. Read, Psalm 35:9. It says, "My soul shall be joyful in the Lord. It shall rejoice in His salvation." Speak it! Believe it! Receive it!

Talk to God! Ask Him to teach you! Pray, "Lord, I want an abundance of joy in my life. I want to know unspeakable joy. I receive Your overflowing waterfall of joy over my life. I thank and praise You for the abundance of joy You bless me with. I know the Spirit of the Lord is upon me. Thank You Jesus for my salvation in the cross!"

Read Psalm 91 and speak these words out loud over your life.

He that dwelleth in the secret place of the most High shall abide under the shadow of the Almighty.

I will say of the Lord, He is my refuge and my fortress: my God; in Him will I trust.

Surely He shall deliver thee from the snare of the fowler, and from the noisome pestilence.

He shall cover thee with His feathers, and under His wings shalt thou trust: His truth shall be thy shield and buckler. Thou shall not be afraid for the terror by night; nor the arrow that flieth by day;

Nor for the pestilence that walketh in the darkness; nor for the destruction that wasteth at noon day.

A thousand shall fall at thy side, and ten thousand at thy right hand; but it shall not come nigh thee.

Only with thine eyes shalt thou behold and see the punishment of the wicked

Because thou hast made the Lord, which is my refuge even the most High, thy habitation;

There shall no evil befall thee, neither shall any plague come nigh thy dwelling.

For He shall give His angels charge over thee, to keep thee in all thy ways.

They shall bear thee up in their hands, lest thou dash thy foot against a stone.

Thou shall tread upon the lion and the adder: the young lion and the dragon shalt thou trample under feet.

Because He has set His love upon me, therefore will I deliver him; I will set him on high because he has known my name.

He shall call upon me, I will answer him, I will be with him in trouble, I will deliver him and honor him.

With long life will I satisfy him, and show him my salvation.

God's protection! His angels have charge over me! No plague comes to my home! No evil befall me! He sets His love upon me! Wow, God you are so awesome! I pray, "Lord I receive all Your words! I thank and praise You for them!"

Let The Healing Begin!

Three Crosses

Chapter 10

There were three crosses on Calvary Hill. Why three, I wondered? Was it because Jesus was denied three times by Peter? Was it that Jesus had asked his disciples three times to stand watch while He prayed at the Garden of Gethsemane. The night Jesus was arrested, Peter was confronted. Someone said, "You know Him, you walk with Jesus." "Oh no, I do not know Jesus," said Peter. Shortly after, Peter denied knowing Jesus two more times.

What were Peter's thoughts as he denied knowing Jesus? Did he fear he would be killed? Did he feel guilty? Did he pray for help? Did he say to himself, "I love Jesus, He is my friend, closer than a brother."

Can you imagine how Jesus felt? He knew Peter would deny Him three times. Have you ever been betrayed by a close friend? You think a friend has your back. The going gets rough, they are gone. How disappointing!

It is easy to have friends when we are having fun. They enjoy being around us. What if we were in trouble? Would our friends help us? If we were in prison would they visit us? Would they still come to see us a year later? If so, they are true friends!

Jesus asked His disciples in the Garden of Gethsemane to sit while He went to pray. Jesus said to them, "My soul is deeply grieved to the point of death. Remain here and keep watch with me." Jesus went a little farther, fell on his face and prayed, "My Father, if it is possible, let this cup pass from me, yet not as I will, but as Your will." Jesus returned to find His disciples sleeping. They had not kept watch.
It had only been an hour.

Jesus, their greatest friend, had said, "Keep watch because my soul is deeply grieved to the point of death." Were they concerned? Did they pray for Jesus? They all fell asleep. Jesus said for a second time, "Keep watch and pray." Jesus went again and prayed, "My Father, if this cannot pass away unless I drink it, Your will be done!"

Jesus returned to find His disciples sleeping again. Then it happened a third time. Jesus said He was deeply grieved! Do you wonder why the disciples never asked, my Lord what is going on? How can we help? Jesus told them what He needed. He asked them to watch and pray. What if the disciples had prayed? Would things have been different for Jesus?

Judas, another disciple and friend, sold out Jesus for thirty pieces of silver. He identified Jesus for the guards by a kiss. He betrayed Jesus! How could Judas have done it? Jesus loved him!

Some friends disappoint us as we go through life. Jesus was perfect in every way. He hand selected His disciples. Some of them saddened His heart by their betrayals. How many times have we disappointed Jesus? We turn away from His word. We get lazy in our walk. We disobey Him. Jesus still continues to forgive us!

There were two thieves on each side of Jesus that day. They heard what was said to Jesus. These men were wicked. They were crucified beside Jesus, King of Kings. Our Savior! They saw Jesus had been beaten until His face was unrecognizable. Jesus was tortured. His hands and feet nailed to the cross. The thieves heard the guards cursing Him and joking. The thieves saw guards gambling for His garments. They saw Him spit on. When Jesus asked for a drink, they saw guards give Him vinegar. They heard Jesus cry out, "Father forgive them, they know not what they do."

What thoughts went through the thieves minds? After all that had been done to Him, Jesus said, "Forgive them!" Did they realize Jesus was the King of the Jews! Did the thieves think because of the beatings, loss of blood and suffering, Jesus did not know what he was saying?

Both thieves witnessed the crucifixion of Jesus. One of the thieves said to Jesus, "Remember me." Jesus said, "Today you will be in paradise!" Jesus did not say, sorry you can't come. You are very wicked. You lived a life of sin. Could it be any plainer! Jesus loves us! Jesus forgives!

Romans 3:23 For all have sinned, and come short of the glory of God.

Three crosses, Jesus and two choices! This was a day about choice! Life or death! Jesus took on the sin of the world. God chose to save all His children! He embraces us! The Lord's love reaches to the Heavens!

II Corinthians 5:17 Therefore if any man be in Christ, he is a new creature; old things are passed away; behold all things are become new.

You can change your life and start enjoying what Jesus has for you! Today, you can receive Jesus into your heart! Repeat these words and accept Him, "Lord Jesus, I ask You to come into my life. Forgive me of all my sins. I denounce satan and all his works. Jesus, You are Lord of my life! I believe You are the Son of God! I believe You died on the cross for my sins! I believe

You rose from the dead on the third day and sit at the right hand of God the Father! Thank You Jesus for saving me! Write my name in the Lambs Book of Life. I pray this all in the name of Jesus!"

Romans 10:13 For whosoever shall call upon the name of the Lord shall be saved.

I John 1:9 If we confess our sins, He is faithful and just to forgive us our sins, and to cleanse us from all unrighteousness.

John 3:16-17 For God so loved the world, that He gave His only begotten Son, that whosoever believeth in Him should not perish but have everlasting life. For God sent not His Son into the world to condemn the world; but that the world through Him might be saved.

I accepted Jesus into my heart when I was five years old. My mom is the one who told me what it meant to be saved. A few months later, I was asked to play the mother of Jesus at the church Christmas Eve service. Wow, what an honor! It was an exciting moment for me, I will never forget it.

I went to church and Sunday school. I learned more about Jesus. The winters are very cold in Minnesota. My dad was not saved at the time. Wherever we lived, my mom, brothers and I walked to church. My Dad would not give us a ride. After we were at the same church for a while, a member would offer to drive us to and from church.

I started going to youth group. It was led by a wonderful youth minister. We had all sorts of wonderful activities. He not only spoke about Jesus, he was a great example of Him.

I will always remember the time when he told us about salvation. He said, "Some of you may be thinking it sounds good, but I don't know that I believe this Jesus stuff." He then added, "Okay, what if you accepted Jesus into your heart. You asked Him to forgive you for your sins. You are already coming to church leading a pretty good life. Then you get to the end of your life and find out it was not true. What are you losing? Now think if you did not accept Jesus. You get to the end of your life and find out it is TRUE! Too late, you burn in hell for eternity!"

It seems the word Christian has become more like a title. If I ask someone if they are a Christian, I still do not know if they are saved. When I ask if they love Jesus, the way they respond makes all the difference!

Jesus suffered, was crucified and died on the cross. Jesus made the sacrifice for us. Receive Him in your heart! Jesus took it all! He paid the price! Start learning! Praying! Reading His word! Get involved and fellowship in a church! **Believe** He is the Son of God! **Know** He is Jesus, King of Kings.

God's People

Chapter 11

Navarre Beach, Florida is located between Destin and Pensacola. I was driving to Pensacola Beach to meet a friend. There were two ways to get there. The most direct and easier route was to take Highway 98 all the way. The other way required some turns and seemed longer. It would take me along a two lane road between Navarre Beach and Pensacola Beach.

I was going to meet for breakfast. Serving time stopped at ten. The direct route seemed to be my best choice. I left my condo early. I allowed plenty of time. As I drove, I prayed for the Lord to go before me, guide my journey and keep me safe. I continued praying about other things. I listened to praise and worship music and a CD of the late great Nat King Cole. What a voice! It was a beautiful day! I was on my way and feeling great!

I passed the turn off to Navarre Beach. I thought, I could go that way. I stopped in a gas station and rechecked my map. I verified it was the turn off. I decided to stay on Highway 98 since it was quicker. I started driving. A short time later, I saw an easy turn around. I thought, I have come this far, I should just continue on 98. I drove on and saw brake lights and traffic stopped ahead. I saw the sign for a toll bridge and thought it was the bridge to Pensacola Beach. I turned onto it, but realized I was driving away from the ocean. I was headed in the wrong direction. I drove to the toll booth. The lady collected my toll. She confirmed I was going the wrong way. Then she said, "I think there is a water main break on 98. You may not be able to cross the bridge to Pensacola Beach."

I drove back to 98 and joined the traffic jam. I moved less than a mile in ten minutes. I still had six more miles to go and only twenty minutes before the breakfast ended. I called my friend and told him to start without me.

As I sat in traffic, I thought about what just happened. I prayed but had not listened. God was speaking! He had been telling me to take another route. The lady at the toll booth said the road might be closed.

We need to listen and pay attention for God's direction when we pray. I needed to turn around. I rolled down my window, smiled and motioned to the car in the next lane over. I made a u-turn and headed back to Navarre. If I had gone that way in the first place, I would have arrived on time.

The sign at the turn off for Navarre read, "Florida's Best Kept Secret." I drove through Navarre and noticed he beautiful Easter egg colored homes. The colors were gorgeous! Bright pink, beautiful orange, baby blue, luscious lavender, sunshine yellow! The front yards were mostly sand, palm trees, sea grass and sea oats. It was like a postcard!

As I drove to Pensacola Beach, I saw white sand dunes. They were amazing but hid the ocean. Suddenly, I had a clear breathtaking view of the water and the sugar sand beaches almost touched the road. Sunlight sparkled on the ocean waves! It was spectacular and continued for miles! I thanked Jesus for this awesome moment! If I had gone the other way, I would have missed it. I would have returned home on 98. I would not have seen the beauty God created!

Later in the day, I went for a walk on the beach. I saw thousands of shells. It was like God was saying, these shells are "My People." They varied in size, shape, and color. All different and unique! The markings on the shells were perfect. Their stripes, patterns and colors were brilliant! I found one shell that my friend told me was rare. I walked a little farther and found a second one. I had only walked a short distance and found a third one. I thought Father, Son, and Holy Spirit! The verse in Ecclesiastes 4:12 came to mind, a cord of three strands is not quickly broken. God said they are all rare, they are all unique, I love them all the same.

I walked farther along the beach. I noticed many little shells clustered together. Suddenly, I saw one shell all by itself. This occurred several times as I walk down the shore line. I thought of the 99 sheep in Luke 15:3-5. Jesus will always go and find the one that is lost. His sheep are all precious to Him. He will place us on His shoulder and carry us, just like that little lamb. Sometimes we stray. We are lost. We are searching in the dark. His lighted way is there for us. Seek Him! Call His name!

I looked at many shells as I walked on the beach. Sometimes the shells that looked the strongest were broken. I thought about the many people who look strong and are breaking inside. Some of the most fragile shells remained intact. I picked one up. It was perfect. No broken pieces or cracks! I thought how did it not break in the rage of a storm?

One night, I was at a church meeting helping an evangelist. She was praying over people who came forward. She began praying for a man who was tall and looked very strong. The Holy Spirit came upon him and he went down on the floor. She said, "Laura go pray over him, God is not done with him." She continued to the next person in line. I knelt down by the man. I put my hand on his arm and started praying quietly. I started weeping. I asked a young girl if she would bring ne some Kleenex. I felt I could not take my hand off his arm. Then I heard God say, "Tell him I know his pain and will heal his heart." I repeated God's message to him. A minister from the church walked over. He put his hand on the man's heart. I knew God healed him!

It does not matter how we appear on the outside. We can be fragile on the inside. Our hearts may be broken by something that occurred years ago. Sometimes we hold onto hurt, anger and bitterness. We keep it inside. Our Heavenly Father is the Healer!

My heart had been broken by the death of my daughter. Many of us suffer from physical or emotional pain. God can heal us when we are hurting if we ask Him. Pray, "In the name of Jesus, I break off the lies of the devil and all negative words I have spoken and others have spoken over me. Remove the pain in my heart and heal my brokenness. Anything not of the Holy Spirit needs to leave now. Jesus, refill me with Your overflowing love, joy, peace, laughter and healing grace. Restore my health and life! Holy Spirit, You live in me! All this I ask in my Heavenly Father's name. Thank You Jesus! I praise Your name! Lord, show me the way and the church to be involved in! The friends I should have in my life! Help me Jesus!" **Jesus knows the problem and He is the answer!**

As I looked at all the shells, they reminded me of hundreds of blessings I have had on my journey. God has placed many people in my life to help me through. My experiences may not have always been what I wanted. Through them I have learned and grown. We can choose to embrace life lessons that challenge us and make them into more than we can imagine! God wants His best for us! I thank God for being in my life! God says we can pray about all things! Trust Him!

I Samuel 16:7 (NKJV)   But the Lord said to Samuel, Do not look at his appearance or at his physical stature, because I have refused him. For the Lord does not see as man sees, or the man looks at the outward appearance, but the Lord looks at the heart."

Philippians 4:7   And the peace of God which passeth all understanding, will guard your hearts and minds through Christ Jesus.

Matthew 22:37-39 Jesus said unto him, thou shall love the Lord thy God with all thy heart and with all thy soul and with all thy mind. This is the first and great commandment. And the second is like unto it, thou shalt love thy neighbor as thyself.

always told my children, "God created you! You create your personality." God commands us to love everyone. Do we open our hearts to bless God's people, to win souls for Jesus? Be ambassadors for Christ!

II Corinthians 5:20 Now then we are ambassadors for Christ, as through God did beseech you by us: we pray you in Christ's stead, be ye reconciled to God.

While finishing this chapter, I learned Andrae Crouch arrived in heaven on January 8, 2015. What a beautiful man! He was a Gospel music pioneer, anointed singer, songwriter, arranger, record producer and loving minister of God. He was loved by all who knew him! His music was a blessing. Every song was a treasure. "Through It All" especially touches my heart. It thanks God for His mountains and valleys and how Jesus brought him through the storms. Andre sang, "For if I never had a problem, I wouldn't know God could solve them. I would never know what **faith in God can do!**"

All of Andre's music is Holy Spirit inspired! It will bless you in a mighty way! He is in the presence of God! In the arms of Jesus! He is dancing and singing on the streets of gold! God has prepared a mansion for him! We can only imagine how he feels!

Matthew 25:21 His Lord said unto him, Well done. thou good and faithful servant: thou has been faithful over a few things, I will make the ruler over many things; enter thou into the joy of thy Lord!

Serve! Be Faithful! Love God!

Blessed In The City

Chapter 12

Deuteronomy 28:1-13

And it shall come to pass, if thou shalt hearken diligently unto the voice of the Lord thy God, to observe and to do all His commandments which I command thee this day, that the Lord thy God will set thee on high above all nations of the earth:

And all these blessings shall come on thee, and overtake thee, if thou shalt hearken unto the voice of the Lord thy God.   Blessed shalt thou be in the city, and blessed shalt thou be in the field.

Blessed shall be the fruit of thy body, and the fruit of thy ground, and the fruit of thy cattle, the increase of thy kine, and the flocks of thy sheep.

Blessed shall be thy basket and thy store.

Blessed shalt thou be when thou comest in, and blessed shalt thou be when thou goest out.

The Lord shall cause thine enemies that rise up against thee to be smitten before thy face: they shall come out against thee one way, and flee before thee seven ways.

The Lord shall command the blessings upon thee in thy storehouses, and in all that thou settest thine hand unto; and He shall bless thee in the land which the Lord thy God giveth thee.

The Lord shall establish thee an holy people unto Himself, and He hath sworn onto thee, if thou shalt keep the commandments of the Lord thy God, and walk in His ways.

And all people of the earth shall see that thou art called by the name of the Lord; and they shall be afraid of thee.

And the Lord shall make the plenteous in goods, in the fruit of thy body, and in the fruit of thy cattle, and in the fruit of thy ground, in the land which the Lord swore unto thy fathers to give thee.

The Lord shall open onto thee His good treasure, the Heaven to give the rain unto thy land in His season, and to bless all the work of thine hand; and thou shalt lend unto many nations, and thou shalt not borrow.

And the Lord shall make thee the head, and not the tail; and thou shall be above only, and thou shalt not be beneath; if that thou hearken unto the commandments of the Lord thy God which I command thee this day, to observe and to do them:

The last verses in Deuteronomy 28:14-68 talk about the curses. And you shalt not go aside from any of the words which I commanded you this day, to the right or the left, to go after other gods to serve them. But it shall come to pass, if thou wilt not hearken unto the voice of the Lord thy God, to observe to do all His commandments and His statue which I commanded thee this day;

that all these curses shall come upon thee and overtake thee..............

We have choices and I choose to follow Jesus! I choose to obey the voice of the Lord my God! I ask for all His blessings, I receive them and I praise and thank Him for all the blessings He has for me. His word says, "All these blessings shall come upon you and overtake you, because you obey the voice of the Lord your God."

God has the power! God wants to bless us! Receive it! For instance, we pray for help. God places someone in our life. They offer to give us help. The first thing we tend to say is, I don't feel comfortable. I couldn't take that, it's too much.

What are we thinking? God puts it in someone's heart to bless us and we refuse it. Are we trying to rob their blessing from God? Doesn't it make you feel good when you help others? We must not deny them the same.

Have you been out to lunch with someone and they wanted to pay the check? Did you argue over the bill? I used to be guilty of being a blessing thief. God told me to stop! I was stealing their blessing. If really torn, give the server a huge tip. Bless them! When someone wants to bless us, receive it. Thank them for blessing you! Blessings are from our Heavenly Father! He loves us!

I John 3:1 (NKJV) Behold what manner of love the Father has bestowed on us, that we should be called children of God! Therefore the world does not know us, because it did not know Him.

Psalm 34:8 O taste and see that the Lord is good: blessed is the man that trusteth in Him.

Proverb 8:35 For whoso findeth me findeth life, and shall obtain favor of the Lord.

Blessings and favor! What do they mean to you? I asked several of my friends what blessings and favor meant to them. They responded as follows:

Unexpected blessings, asking and giving His favor. Blessing and giving us favor are one in the same. God is looking upon us in a special way.

God granting favor to fulfill His purpose as He did with Joseph. He found favor in the sight of God. I'm blessed and favored deeply in His love.

A blessed day, the Lord is by my side in all things. To be still and listen to God's plan for me.

Blessings start with God's grace. Favor is when we are fully surrendered.

People had favor with God in the Bible. For example, when the angel spoke to Mary and said she was highly favored by God.

Favor is God's promptings inside the blessings to work for His purpose. It's like the flour and chocolate chip in the cookies.

My friends, children of the King, described what blessings and favor meant to them. Their answers varied. Your answer may be different also. It is amazing how one question can result in so many varying responses. God talks about favor and blessings all through His Word. I clearly see everyone knows favor and blessings from God are indescribably delicious and wonderful to receive!

Psalm 103:1-5 Bless the Lord, O my soul: and all that is within me, bless His Holy name. Bless the Lord, O my soul, and forget not all His benefits. Who forgiveth all thine iniquities; Who healeth it all thy diseases; Who redeemeth thy life from destruction; Who crowned thee with loving kindness and tender mercies. Who satisfieth thy mouth with good things; so that thy youth is renewed like the eagle's.

I've heard people say, "I read the Bible but don't really understand it." I have said those words in the past. It may be better to start with verses or a chapter. Ask God for His Holy Spirit Wisdom and Understanding!

James 1:5 (NKJV) If any of you lacks wisdom, let him ask of God, Who gives to all liberally and without reproach, and it will be given to him.

God knows each of us individually. He knows our needs through His Spirit. He gives us our own answers. When we do not know the answer, we need to seek Him! Ask Him! God's answer is not in our timing, it is in His. We read the Bible, but we may not receive the understanding right away. I have learned that in order to understand God's word, we must invite the Holy Spirit into our hearts! He will teach us all things!

John 14:26-27 (NKJV) But the Helper, the Holy Spirit, whom the Father will send in My name, He will teach you all things, and bring to your remembrance all things that I said to you. Peace I leave with you, My peace I give to you; not as the world gives do I give you. Let not your heart be troubled, neither let it be afraid.

Be open for the Holy Spirit! We may read something in the Bible and not comprehend it. Acts chapter 2:1-4 talks about the day of Pentecost, speaking in other tongues and that the Spirit gave them utterance. Sometimes we do not understand and say, "Not for me."

Instead pray, "Holy Spirit give me knowledge and understanding of this. Your Word says You can teach me all things." It is often the same in life. We want to learn something new and unfamiliar. We may not understand it. The more we educate ourselves, the more we grow and learn. There are several books written about the Holy Spirit. The one that helped me grow and learn was, "The New You & The Holy Spirit" by Andrew Wommack.

We don't want to limit God in us. We want to be led by God's Word through His Holy Spirit. Keep your mind, heart, soul and spirit open to the leading of the Holy Spirit!

Blessed In The City!

In Closing

In closing, I wanted to share these words from Jesse Duplantis. Jesse is a dynamic evangelist, called to minister God's message. I believe it is a good ending for my book and a great beginning for the new chapters in your life!

Jesse Duplantis has a TV ministry. I heard him say this in February 2011. "I love Star Trek, I've loved it from the day it was created, I like It, I don't know why. Space, the final frontier. These are the voyages of the Star Ship Enterprise. It's a five year mission. You know it, but I had to change it. Ministry the final frontier, these are the voyages of the Children of God. Our lifelong mission is to seek out new souls for His Glory and Honor, to fill new hearts with His presence and power to teach the uncompromised Word of God. To boldly go where Jesus Christ tells us to go, live long and prosper!"

We are all children of God! Share His Word! Win souls for Christ!

Walk Boldly On Water With Jesus!

Acknowledgments

No one gets where they are by themselves. All the places I have been, all the people I have met, my experiences, family, friendships, job, and travel have all helped to mold and shape my life. The lessons, burdens, joy and tears have all completed me. Yes, like most of us, I have had people in my life who hurt or treated me poorly. Some have tried to rob me of my peace and come between God and me. I cannot let the bad distract me or take away my focus on Jesus. I have become smarter and learned from my mistakes.

I surround myself with the people God places in my life. My incredible family that you were introduced to in this book. I have moved often in the last few years. My family has been fully supportive of my several moves. They repeatedly say, "What do you need? We are here for you!"

I have several extraordinary lifelong friends. I also have friends I have met and felt like I had known all my life. God placed each one of them to help or complete my journey.

I am blessed with God's treasures from Heaven! Those blessings of love, help, and generosity are not taken for granted. I am proud of the wonderful examples

Acknowledgments

my family and friends are! Tears fill my eyes when I think of how special they are and how they bless me!

May God bestow love, peace, joy and blessings upon each of you! I Love you all!

Contributions

I think of all the ministers and teachers that have spoken into my life over the years. I am thankful there were many. They spoke words of God into my life, helping me learn and grow. I remember hearing Billy Graham speak for the first time at age thirteen. My neighbor friend wanted to accept Christ, and I went forward with him.

My mom, a true prayer warrior. She always told me I was an overcomer. She believed in me and loved me unconditionally. My mom set the bar high with the example how she lived her life.

To all the ministers, teachers, and staff at Charis Bible College. I will be forever grateful for the knowledge you have passed on to me. Your generosity of time and caring ways helped make a difference in my life. Know that your actions and words taught me to be a disciple for Jesus! You blessed me! Thank you!

Walk on Water Artist, Music and Lyrics

Thank you, to Daniel, Rick, and Tom! Mighty men of God! Your extraordinary accomplishments amaze me! Your Holy Spirit words fill me with joy! You reflect the Glory of God! Heavenly Blessings on your life!

Daniel Garza

Daniel was born in Fresno, California and raised in Texas. He attended Texas A&M University where he majored in music and education. Daniel is a full-time high school teacher, singer, songwriter, recording artist, accomplished studio musician and worship leader for two churches in Corpus Christi, Texas. He is a member of the Corpus Christi Jazz ensemble and also appears as a solo artist. Daniel performed all the vocals and instruments heard on the Walk on Water CD. He also shared in the writing of lyrics and music. Daniel can be reached on Facebook, by email Danielgarzamusic@yahoo.com Website@DanielGarzaMusic.com

Rick Hoefel

Rick is a Texas songwriter by the way of St. Louis, Missouri and Los Angeles California. Rick writes

Christian, country and other genres of music. He is a member of BMI and Nashville Songwriters Association International. His talents and abilities have taken him through many mighty waters. I will be forever grateful for his patience and many hours editing this book. He shared his song writing talents with me. I could have not accomplished the Walk on Water CD by myself. Rick can be contacted by email at; Saltwatersongwriter@yahoo.com or website: SaltwaterSongwritermusic.com

Tom Hoefel

Tom is a singer and songwriter, Tom lives in the hill country of Texas with his lovely wife. He is one half of the music duo, "Cool Waters." Brothers, Tom and Rick have written several songs together including "Put your Life in My Hands." It is another amazing God song! How wonderful to have so much talent in the family! These brothers took similar career paths. Now they both journey down the road of music. I am very blessed they have crossed my path!

Laura Charlene

No, I am not a singer or a musician. Yet, I shared in the writing of the lyrics for the CD, "Walk on Water. I heard God whisper, "Laura get out of the boat and follow me!" When we journey with God, He will take us places we cannot imagine. Some days I feel like I'm on a jet ski or behind the wheel of a racing boat! Other times I am floating or sailing calmly along with the soft sea breeze blowing through my hair and the warm sun on my face. God had me writing the words to these songs long before I knew there would be a music CD. I could have said," I can't write. I can't read a note." God already knew that! Instead, I answered His call and started putting ideas to paper! He makes a way in the mighty waters! These songs are the result! I asked, Jesus what is next for me? I am available. I am putting on my running shoes so I can keep up! I'm excited and looking forward to the plans God has for me!

To download each song from the Walk On Water CD,

please visit: www.lauracharlene.com

Put My Life In Your Hands
Prayer Parts Waters
Bridge That Cross
Walk on Water

The following are the lyrics for the songs on CD, "Walk on Water."

Put My Life In Your Hands

Never been one to dive in head first
Afraid to take that step
Riding the fence between faith and the flesh
Has made my life a mess
This time You are the difference
I've finally learned to trust

Chorus

I put my life in Your Hands
Know where I've been, who I am
Only You feel how much I hurt
Been waiting on me to say these words
Let the Spirit fill my soul
I give up all control
Please forgive all of my sins
I put my life in Your hands
Through You all things are possible

Just look at how I've changed
Now I can't wait for dawn to break
To see where I'm led each day
You have made all the difference
Given me so much

    I put my life in Your hands
    Know where I've been, who I am
    Only You feel how much I hurt
    I'll follow Your Holy Word
    Let the Spirit fill my soul
    I give up all control
    You took on all of my sins
    I put my life in Your hands

Bridge

Love me, touch me, God I live my life for You
    I put my life in Your hands
    You are the great I Am
    Washed away my guilt and hurt
    I'm sharing Your Holy Word
    Let the Spirit fill my soul
    I give up all control
    You took on all my sins
    I put my life in Your hands
    Put your life in His hands

@2013

Prayer Parts Waters

I couldn't hold back the tidal wave
Of problems brought on by my mistakes
Fell to my knees, You forgave
Covered me in Your grace, I've been saved

    Prayer parts waters
    Prayer empowers
    In the darkest hours
    You're always there
    You answer prayer
    With loving care
    When souls are bared
    Prayer parts waters

You give new life, turn water to wine
Dark skies give way to bright sunshine
No ocean too deep, river too wide
Through prayer You change despair to divine

Chorus
Bridge

    Prayer parts waters
    Prayer empowers
    In the darkest hours
    You're always there

You answer prayer
With loving care
When souls are bared
Prayer parts waters

Don't give up give praise
Look up in faith and pray
Rise up and give thanks
What a difference our God makes
Chorus

Prayer parts waters
Prayer empowers
In the darkest hours
You're always there
You answer prayer
With loving care
When souls are bared
Prayer parts waters
Prayer parts waters
Prayer parts waters
@2015

Bridge That Cross

Wasn't the water that was troubled
He was teetering on the edge of no return
Hungry, tired, puzzled, lost in the shuffle
Cried out, Lord save me from my struggle

    When it seemed all was lost
    He bridged that cross
    Homeless shelter, meal, hot bath
    Jesus paid the cost
    So he could bridge that cross
    Gave him back his pride
    Started a new life
    He came to it, he bridged that cross

She bore the scars from the last time it happened
He was missing his meetings, drinking again
With every second, she felt more threatened
Prayed for the Lord's shield of protection
Chorus

    When it seemed all was lost
    She bridged that cross
    Women's shelter, caring staff
    Jesus paid the cost
    So she could bridge that cross
    Gave her back her pride

Started a new life

She came to it, she bridged that cross
Pink ribbon, deep loss, disasters, laid off
Broken heart, bad thoughts, final chapter, last
straw
We'll find ourselves at the foot of the cross

Chorus

    When it seems all is lost
    It's time to bridge that cross
    Shelter in a love that's unsurpassed
    Jesus paid the cost
    So we can bridge that cross
    Give up our pride
    Start a whole new life
    Come to Him, bridge that cross
    Come to Him, bridge His cross
@2014

Walk on Water

Fishermen pulled in their nets
Storm was causing their unrest
Jesus appeared loving arms outstretched
Called to Peter, "Come take that step"

Peter gave in to the wind and waves
Jesus said, "Ye of little faith"
"I am the Way. Don't be afraid"
Reached out His hand
Peter was saved

Get out of the boat
    Trust in our Father
    He's given us hope
    Walk on water
    Get out of the boat
    We're granted the power
    He'll keep us afloat
    Walk on water

We complain and blame it on fate
Any excuse to play it safe
Pray for answers, but don't want to change
He's already shown us the way

Get out of the boat
    Trust in our Father
    He's given us hope
    Walk on water
    Get out of the boat
    We're granted the power
    He'll keep us afloat
    Walk on water

Jesus offers us His hand
He's our lighthouse, our life raft
His plan leads to the shores of Heaven
Take that step, be fishers of men

Get out of the boat
    Trust in our Father
    He's given us hope
    Walk on water
    Get out of the boat
    We're granted the power
    He'll keep us afloat
    Walk on water
    Walk on water Walk on water
    Walk on water
@2014

References

BrainyQuotes.com

ChristianQuotes.com

Christian-Quotes.OChristians.com

Dictionary.Com – www.dictionary.com

Jesse Duplantis - www.JDM.org

Steve Harvey Act Like A Success Think Like A Success
(September 2014 – Trinity Broadcasting Network)

Carman Licciardello - www.carman.org
Carman Licciardello Face Book
Carman Licciardello CD, "No Plan B"
Carman Licciardello - Battling Cancer, Interview by
Turning Point April 16, 2014

Dr. Terry Mortenson, Noah's Flood Washing Away
Millions Of Year

Andrew Wommack You've Already Got It (November 2006)
God Wants You Well (July 2010)
The New You and the Holy Spirit (September 2012)
Andrew Wommack Ministries – www.awmi.net
Charis Bible Collegewww.charisbiblecollege.org

Made in the USA
Columbia, SC
24 May 2019